"On a damaged earth, human beings must finally learn to meet more-than-humans on their terms. That's no small trick for the vertebrate-centric, especially when the partners are unfamiliars like diatoms and slugs. Helped by one or two spirit familiars, this smart, lively book is full of tips for cultivating response-ability, possibly even before the dire heritage of human exceptionalism boils us all up."

–**Donna Haraway**, *Professor Emerita, History of Consciousness and Feminist Studies, University of California, Santa Cruz, USA*

"A sensitive yet vibrant and sympathetically weird volume exploring queer ways to think of the less emphasized others of our world's occupants. The authors remind us that posthumanism deals with a host of alien and strange fabulations which have lived alongside us and existed for longer than us, in their own ways irreducible to anthropocentric philosophical capture. A beautiful and activism-inspiring book."

–**Patricia MacCormack**, *Professor of Continental Philosophy, Anglia Ruskin University, Cambridge, UK*

"With tenderness and vulnerability, the authors sincerely stretch their hands, hearts, and minds out to meet and be met by alien others. In doing so they sculpt a post-human practice of kinship that is much needed in these petro-patriarchal times. Playful, thoughtful, and committed, this book bridges theory, art, and creative writing, putting to use all these tools in such a way that readers will feel they can embark on alien journeys themselves."

–**Camila Marambio**, *PhD, Curator, Artist, Independent Researcher, Ensayos. Curator of the Chilean Pavillion Turba Tol Hol-Hol at the 59th Venice Art Biennale 2022*

"This book is a kin-spirited gathering of somatic and spectral desires to connect with mineralized, mucous-abundant, and mysterious others beyond, and within, our different Earthly ways of being. It seeks out creative, epistemic hybridity through collective imaginings that tenderly nibble and glide, and poetically disrupt genres of writing, knowing, care, and companionability with other-than-human collaborators."

–**Susan Reid**, *PhD, University of Sydney, Australia, Cultural Theorist, Creative Researcher, Artist, and Writer*

"Overturning expectations, the authors playfully and deconstructively employ both cognitive and affective techniques of estrangement and defamiliarization to undermine human exceptionalism and power, offering instead radically different, mutualistic practices of more-than-human companionships. For many readers, this startling and ambitious text will be an alien – yet highly productive – encounter in itself."

–**Margrit Shildrick**, *Guest Professor of Gender and Knowledge Production, Stockholm University, Sweden*

Feminist Reconfigurings of Alien Encounters

Feminist Reconfigurings of Alien Encounters reclaims the notion of alien encounters together with strange but queerly loved companions: Vulgar slugs, diatoms (micro-algae), and familiars (spirit guides of witches). The book's three human co-authors ask: what would it take to establish more-than-human, bio- and geo-egalitarian co-existence on a planet in trouble?

This playfully crafted mixed-genre book is informed by feminist posthumanisms and co-created with a spectral community of more-than-humans who are respectfully summoned to contribute with their perspectives. In focus of the entangled artistic-philosophical-poetic investigations are questions of ethics, aesthetics, and methodologies to co-exist response-ably rather than based on modern human beliefs in exceptionalism and entitlement to sovereignty, control, and conquest of more-than-human worlds.

Feminist Reconfigurings of Alien Encounters is intended for broad global audiences of researchers, teachers, professionals, NGOs, politicians, students from undergraduate to postgraduate levels, artists, writers, activists, and artivists who are interested in entangled artistic-poetic-philosophical modes of understanding the world as well as in ecology, new feminist materialism, critical posthumanism, and questions about radically rethinking and reimagining human/more-than-human relations on Earth.

Nina Lykke is Professor Emerita, Gender Studies, Linköping University, Sweden, and Aarhus University, Denmark, and a poet and writer. Her research focuses on queer death studies, intersectionality, feminist posthumanism, and queer ecologies. Her monographs include *Cosmodolphins* (2000), *Feminist Studies* (2010), and *Vibrant Death* (2022).

Katja Aglert is a Stockholm-based artist and 2020–2022 Professor of Art, Linköping University, Sweden. For 20 years, she has explored transdisciplinary, often collaborative processes situated in feminist and more-than-human imaginaries. Her exhibitions include FLORA ars + natura, Bogotá; Marabouparken, Stockholm; Museum of Contemporary Art, Santiago de Chile.

Line Henriksen is Senior Lecturer in Literature and Creative Writing at Malmö University, Sweden. She is the author of the monograph *In the Company of Ghosts: Hauntology, Ethics, Digital Monsters* (2016), and her research interests include monster theory, hauntology, and creative writing as method.

More Than Human Humanities
Recent titles in series:

Extracting Reconciliation
Indigenous Lands, (In)human Wastes, and Colonial Reckoning
Myra J. Hird and Hillary Predko

Feminist Reconfigurings of Alien Encounters
Ethical Co-Existence in More-than-Human Worlds
Nina Lykke, Katja Aglert and Line Henriksen

For more information about this series, please visit: www.routledge.com/
More-Than-Human-Humanities/book-series/MTHH

Feminist Reconfigurings of Alien Encounters

Ethical Co-Existence in More-than-Human Worlds

Nina Lykke, Katja Aglert, and Line Henriksen

Routledge
Taylor & Francis Group

LONDON AND NEW YORK

First published 2024
by Routledge
4 Park Square, Milton Park, Abingdon, Oxon OX14 4RN

and by Routledge
605 Third Avenue, New York, NY 10158

Routledge is an imprint of the Taylor & Francis Group, an informa business

© 2024 Nina Lykke, Katja Aglert and Line Henriksen

The right of Nina Lykke, Katja Aglert and Line Henriksen to be identified as authors of this work has been asserted in accordance with sections 77 and 78 of the Copyright, Designs and Patents Act 1988.

British Library Cataloguing-in-Publication Data
A catalogue record for this book is available from the British Library

ISBN: 978-1-032-44756-8 (hbk)
ISBN: 978-1-032-44757-5 (pbk)
ISBN: 978-1-003-37376-6 (ebk)

DOI: 10.4324/9781003373766

Typeset in Times New Roman
by Apex CoVantage, LLCs

Contents

    Internal Editor as Familiar Spirit**   61
    LINE HENRIKSEN

5   **More-than-Human Ethics and Poetics**   75
    NINA LYKKE

6   **Conversations on Alien Methods and Writing**   93
    KATJA AGLERT AND LINE HENRIKSEN

    Epilogue: Endless End   *109*
    Nina Lykke, Katja Aglert, and Line Henriksen
    References   *116*
    Index   *123*

Acknowledgements

First of all, we want to express a deepfelt thanks to Marietta Radomska, Linköping University. This book would not have come about without all the enthusiastic interventions of Marietta, who for several years was part of our Alien Encounters Writing Collective, which, among others, produced the poetic Intertexts of the book. We lack words to express how important your presence in our collective work on the book has been – first as a regular group member and later, when you had to leave the group for work-related reasons but continued to be spectrally present at our meetings as one of our key writing companions. Marietta, your never-tiring enthusiasm for everything more-than-human, your brilliant eco-philosophical thinking, and your summoning of yet another amazing alien figure, the holobiont lichen, have been an immense inspiration for our work.

We are also grateful that you, in your capacity of series co-editor – together with Cecilia Åsberg – invited us to contribute to the More-than-Human Humanities book series at Routledge. We thank you wholeheartedly, Marietta and Cecilia, for hosting our book in your wonderful series.

We also want to warmly thank other spectral presences in the Alien Encounters Writing Collective that crafted this book, namely the three other-than-human figures, Vulgar slugs (*Arion vulgaris*), the micro-algae, diatoms, and the familiars of witches, whom we have summoned to be our writing companions. Even though we do not know, if you, Slug, Diatom, and Familiar, appreciate to be summoned the way in which we have done it, we want to thank you all very warmly for your guidance. We have tried to do our very best to co-become with you while writing this book. However, we are only humans, so, please, bear with us. It is likely that we were not able to fully learn the lessons you were teaching us. Still, we hope you find that our modes of trying are aligned with your efforts to co-shape worlding practices which are better than the necropolitical ones governing the contemporary world.

As more occasional but still crucial participants in the spectral circles that at various points in time have taken part in the activities of our Alien Encounters Writing Collective, we also want to very warmly thank Tara Mehrabi, who summoned allergy-generating pollen, and Camila Marambio, who summoned the mistletoe to writing sessions that were crucial for the unfolding of the thoughts and sensibilities on more-than-human encounters, which eventually led to this book.

Moreover, warm thanks go to organizers and participants of the Alien Encounters seminars and workshops at Linköping University (April 2018), at KTH, The Royal Institute of Technology, Stockholm (June 2019), and at the Multispecies Storytelling in Intermedial Practices conference, Linnéus University, Växjö (January 2019). Special thanks to Marietta Radomska, Cecilia Åsberg, Veera Weetzel, and Janna Holmstedt, co-organizers of the Stockholm event, and Ida Bencke and Jørgen Bruhn, who organized the Växjö conference.

Thanks also to our anonymous Routledge reviewers for enthusiasm and inspiring comments, as well as to Routledge commissioning editor Charlotte Taylor and editorial assistant Jodie Collins for useful help and support.

We also want to thank the island of Fur in Limfjorden, Denmark, for hosting amazing writing retreats and for framing and giving shape to the corpo-affecting magic which is necessary for individual as well as collective writing.

In addition to deep-felt collective thanks to all those we have mentioned above, each of us wants to express special thanks to human and more-than-human beings who have supported us in the writing of this book.

Katja would like to sincerely thank Ted von Proschwitz for the continuous scientific guidance in the gastropod worlds. A heartfelt thank-you to Geoff Robinson for the support and conversation in relation to the writing of my slug chapter. A warm thank-you to Charlotte Bydler, Tora Holmberg, Katarina Wadstein MacLeod, and Camila Marambio. Thank you to Marietta Radomska and Cecilia Åsberg, who invited me to be part of seminars at Linköping University, which eventually – thanks to Marietta and Nina Lykke – led to the Alien Encounters project. Thank you, every person in the audiences of the lecture performances related to Vulgar slugs that I have been performing over the years. Their comments, participation, and questions have meant so much for my thinking and work in the Alien Encounters project and beyond. A heartfelt thank you, Marietta, for the collaboration and friendship. Thank you to my family, with special thanks to Nadia and Ramona and to Carin and Runo. Thank you to my lovely friends who showed so much excitement and support in their joint interest for slugs and snails. Thank you so very much to my dear human companions in the Alien Encounters project, Line and Nina. It has been and still is an amazing transformative journey. Thank you, dear slugs and snails, for prompting me to pay closer attention. Finally, a deep heartfelt thank you to Oskar Aglert for your love and excitement during the countless times I have stopped during our walks to spend time with slugs and snails.

Line would like to thank Katja, Nina, and Marietta for many exciting years of alien encounters. Also a heartfelt thank-you to writing coach Mirjam Godskesen for your generosity and guidance, which helped me finish this and other writing projects. Thank you to my lovely colleagues at Medea Lab – Hugo Boothby, Lucy Cathcart Frödén, Martin Cathcart Frödén, Erin Corey, Magnus Denker, Bo Reimer, and Bojana Romic – for building and nurturing such a supportive environment for weird thoughts and ideas. A special thank-you to you, Bo, for all your support during my first years at Malmö University. Thank you to Margrit Shildrick, as always and for everything (but especially for the cat pictures)! Thank you, Katrine Meldgaard Kjær, for wonderful writing-collabs that taught me so much, and thank you, writing buddies

Aino-Kaisa Koistinen, Astrid Møller-Olsen, Chera Kee, Erika Kvistad, Louise Bang Olesen, and Megen de Bruin-Molé, for moral support, gifs, and so, so many pomodoros. Thank you, Camilla Gerhardt, for old friendship and new adventures. A great big thank-you to my parents, Hanne and Claus Henriksen, and my sister, Louise, for the love, support, and patience. Thank you, søssi, for the pictures for the collages! A final, crucial thank-you to Inga and Konrad for being such good dogs and to Nigel for being such a terrible help.

I (Nina) would like to thank all those who guided me towards bonding with aliens rather than rejecting them. First of all, warm thanks to you, Magnus, white albino laboratory rat with red eyes and pink tail, rescued from lab death and given to seven-year-old me in 1956 as a beloved pet by my medical researcher stepfather. Magnus, I loved you when you ran around in my childhood room and bed, biting hundreds of little holes in my duvet and cleverly making a lot of noise gnawing on dry bread when you wanted to tell me that I should give you more exciting food than that. Your beautiful pink tail immensely frightened schoolmates visiting me, and I truly did not understand why they considered your beautiful tail to be abject. Magnus, I still remember the touch of your soft white fur and your hairless tail on my body, and I think the queer companionship I developed with you, Magnus, in my early childhood, is the foundation of all my later posthuman queerness. I also want to thank warmly my beloved lesbian life partner, Mette Bryld, who passed away in 2014. Mette, without your exceptional love and amazing way of guiding me towards the queer stories of dolphin–human relations, which we explored as part of the writing of our co-authored book *Cosmodolphins* (2000), I could not have engaged in this book on alien encounters. Warm-warm thanks, my forever and ever beloved! Looking forward to reconnecting with your ashes in the diatomite surroundings on the bottom of Limfjorden! I also want to thank you, my dear, dear friend, Camila Marambio. Your spontaneous embrace of a beautiful one-meter-high flowering thistle, whose humble weed existence the riverside managers of my hometown, Odense, for unknown reasons had spared the first summer you visited me here, made an indelible impression on me. Later, you opened my eyes to the life of mistletoe, peatmoss, and peatlands. Warm thanks, dearest Camila. Very warm thanks also goes to you, my dear tortie cat, Musse, who so gracefully taught me about the pleasures of cat–human skin contact when cultivating the habit of putting the hairless part of your paw against my fingertips. Thanks also to all you minute diatom friends – fossilized and alive in the waters around Fur. Finally, thanks to you, dear Line and dear Katja, for an amazing collaboration and for a friendship that I hope will last beyond this book. Warm thanks also to you, dear Marietta, for your amazing contributions to this book and for all our other collaborations, which I sincerely hope will continue for a long, long time. Finally, I want warmly to thank both of you, Marietta Radomska and Cecilia Åsberg, for hosting our book in your Routledge book series on More-than-Human Humanities.

July 2023
Nina Lykke
Katja Aglert
Line Henriksen

Figures

Figure 0.1 Triquetra.
Source: © Katja Aglert 2023.

Figure 0.2 Alien Encounters – Triquetra. Collage created for this publication based on
      photographs by the three authors of this volume.

Source: © Katja Aglert 2023.

Prologue

Experimental Writing with Spectral Communities and Triquetras

Nina Lykke, Katja Aglert, and Line Henriksen

Line: How do you begin writing a prologue?

Katja: Well, you can ask a moon card – a deck of oracle cards (Boland 2018) that I often use to guide me in demanding situations. I draw three cards from the deck and see what they advise me to do. Let's see what the cards say about the prologue to this book about feminist reclaiming of alien encounters:

A fiery climax approaches!
It is time to take action!
Take time to breathe out!

Nina: Oh, such a clear message. The feminist reclaiming of the alien encounter is a fiery climax to come, urging us to take action against human alienation from each other and from the more-than-human world, and after that, breathe out and take a moment to relax together with all the amazing critters of the planet . . . Isn't this basically what our book is about?

A Fiery Climax Approaches: When Triquetras Meet

This book is written by three human co-authors, Nina, Katja and Line, sometimes together, sometimes separately, and often in conversation with what we have come to understand as our "alien figures": Vulgar slugs, the micro-algae diatoms, and familiars (witches' spirit helpers). Together with the three alien figures, we critically rethink the concept of alien encounters and try to reconfigure what it means to practice them while trying to engage in alternative, mutually enriching rather than exploitative modes. We explore what such encounters can do to our understanding of more-than-human companionships on a vulnerable planet, as well as – on a more personal level – what role our alien figures can and do play in our lives, writing, and ethico-political practices.

Due to the mirrored "three" – the three human co-authors and the three "alien figures" – one of the anonymous reviewers of our initial book proposal suggested the figure of the triquetra as a means of teasing out this structure. We are grateful for this suggestion. With its use within witchcraft and pagan spiritual practices, the triquetra serves as a scaffold or framework for some of the thoughts and ideas that went into our writing of this book. That is, attempts at thinking beyond Western rationalism and paradigms, beyond the framework for what can "reasonably" be said to exist, and exist as worthy of ethical consideration and creative companionship.

The triquetra is a symbolic figure, consisting of three vesica pisces (almond shaped figures), superimposed so that the lines indicating their contours move endlessly into each other, see Figure 0.1 (Wikipedia 2023b). Vesica pisces (literally translated into fish vessels) symbolize the vulva. The triquetra has a complex cultural history and appears in many contexts (in Europe and in Eastern as well as Western parts of Asia). First of all, it is to be considered as an ancient symbol for the tripartite goddess (Walker 1988). This goddess figure, who is known in many shapes all over the globe (Abendroth 2012), embodies the trinity of seasons (spring, summer, and autumn/winter, which in premodern agrarian cultures in temperate and subtropical climates were spiritually and materially related to the cyclic life, death, and rebirth of plants); the trinity of moon phases (the waxing moon, the full moon, and the waning moon that was important for lunar calendars); the trinity of earth zones (heaven, earth, and underworld); and the trinity of feminine powers and wisdom (connected to the ages of youth, maturity, and old age (Bachofen [1861] 1967; Graves 1961; Göttner-Abendroth 1980, 2012).

This ancient Goddess related trinity was appropriated, transformed, and patriarchalized by Christianity, and the triquetra is therefore also sometimes called the "trinity knot" and even "the Celtic trinity knot" due to a culturally visible relation to Celtic culture and a strong presence in Ireland (see, for example, Irish Around the World 2023). It is found as ornamentation on tombstones in graveyards in Ireland, as part of the Celtic cross, as well as in ancient Irish gospel books such as the ninth-century AD *Book of Kells* in Trinity College, Dublin (Wikipedia 2023b). In spite of these Christian/Catholic references, the triquetra is considered to be both older than Christianity and globally much more widespread due to its close symbolic kinship with the ancient tripartite goddess. Albeit repressed, the ancient pagan beliefs related to the triquetra symbol continued to exist in submerged traditions of resistance to the Christian church and were embodied, among others, in the occult practices of witches and sorcerers who were violently persecuted and burned at the stake in many parts of Europe in early modernity. In a short historical account of European occulture, posthumanist feminist philosopher Patricia MacCormack (2020, 110–137) traces the queer aspects of this "vulvic" resistance of all kinds of demonized, monstrous, untameable, and abjectified bodies which did not fit the gender-binary and patriarchal schemes that were institutionalized by church and state as part of the emergence of European modernity and colonial capitalism.

In this volume, we adopt the triquetra to reclaim genealogies between present-day posthumanist critiques of the human/non-human and nature/culture divides and indigenous and a-modern philosophies and pagan spiritualities, which were alive also in Europe until erased by modernity, as the folktales (Göttner-Abendroth 1980) and the history of witchcraft and occulture testify to (Federici 2004). We agree with indigenous posthumanists (Todd 2016; Schaeffer 2018), who emphasize that critical posthumanism should recognize its indebtedness to indigenous thought and take genealogies in a-modern and pagan philosophies thoroughly into account instead of pretending that onto-epistemological undoing of human/non-human and nature/culture divides is its invention.

As manifested in Figure 0.2, we have specifically summoned the triquetra into our book to help us spell out the spiritual-material bonds and companionships that we (the three human co-authors) have tried to shape up and unfurl through our collaborative writing experiments and our ongoing individual as well as collective conversations with the three "alien figures". However, we agree with Patricia MacCormack when she underlines that it is important to avoid "fetishistic appropriation" of occult and spiritual practices from other places and times (2020, 110). We should be painstakingly aware that such practices are part of "ancient and seriously-adhered-to traditions" (Ibid.), whose contexts and meanings should be carefully respected for the ways in which they embody wisdom and insights that cannot, just like that, be incorporated in the modern modes of thinking with which we (the three human co-authors) have grown up. Our use of the triquetra should therefore be understood as experimental, tentative, and emergent, that is, considered as a magical framework, which may or may not lead to more-than-human networking, community building, and shared action. Each of the human co-authors summons an alien figure into the book with whom she has had a prior alien encounter. From this point of departure, she tries to engage the two other co-authors as well as the two other alien figures in an extended triquetra-like companionship, but the outcome is open-ended.

It is Time to Take Action: Writing with Spectral Communities

Writing is always collaborative, and sometimes, these collaborations are easily noticeable, such as when several co-authors are listed on the cover of a book, and sometimes – as Line points out (Chapter 6, this volume) – they are more spectral. By spectral collaborative writing, we refer to how no work and no texts spring from nothingness, but is in conversation with the ideas of others, whether artists, theorists, colleagues, friends, alien figures, moon cards, internal critics (see Chapter 4, this volume), etc., that is, people, aliens, and other creatures who are less directly involved in the writing, but whose absence is felt as a haunting trace throughout the finished text (see also The Monster Network 2021). In this way, we see a call and time for action as not only about the individual (human) subject but also about multiplicities and collectives not always easily distinguishable or categorizable to the human observer – perhaps because they move at paces difficult for the human subject to appreciate (such as the travels of slugs or the slow, careful work of millennia that shape diatomite cliffs) or across spectrums of reality deemed unworthy of serious consideration (the spell-work of familiars).

In our case, the spectral writing collectivity has been at play in our collaboration with our present absent (Derrida 1994) alien figures – diatoms, familiars, and slugs – but also with other people. One of our most important spectral collaborators is Marietta Radomska, who was initially part of the "alien encounters" project, and whose ideas, thoughts and creativity have helped shape this book. It was also Marietta who suggested that we do this book for Routledge's More-Than-Human Humanities series, which she co-edits together with Cecilia Åsberg. Another example of spectral collectivity at work in this volume are the collages, which are based on a collection of photographs gathered by the three authors and crafted by Katja. In short, whether the chapters of this book are authored by one of us, two of us, or three of us, we acknowledge that spectral collective writing has been part of the whole book.

The book is a reflection on and exploration of our encounters with our own "aliens" but also with how we have been and continue to be alien to ourselves and each other. In many ways, the book is a reflection on work relationships and friendships that have developed over several years, making us characters in an unfolding story about alien encounters. This means that we weave in and out of each other's stories in this book, sometimes as (co)narrator(s), sometimes as the supporting character of someone else's story. This is perhaps most visible in Intertexts I–III (Alien Arrivals), which can be described as assemblages of text fragments, poems, and stories created from writing exercizes using automatic writing, and based on our respective alien figures: slugs, diatoms, and familiars. The Alien Arrivals texts precede Chapters 2, 3, and 4, in which we also reflect on the creation of these collaborative texts. This means that we, to some extent, have approached each other's texts as "objects of analysis", both analyzing and reflecting on each other's narratives. To some of us, this was a somewhat alien experience, as our "selves" were returned to us through the eyes of someone else, making what we thought familiar strange (for more on this alien "looking back", see also Nina's poem "And the Animals Noticed Us" in Chapter 5, this volume).

Take Time to Breathe Out: Releasing This Book to Its Own Encounters

At the moment of writing this prologue, we are readying the manuscript for publication and both looking back – trying to describe the process leading up to now – and forward towards a future in which we have released this book into (hopefully) strange futures where it might encounter aliens of its own. As you may see when reading the different stories in this book, alien encounters can indicate "a moment to relax together", as Nina mentions at the beginning of this prologue, and it can mean the opposite; in our experience, remaining open to the alien encounter can be both pleasurable and challenging, joyous and anxiety-inducing, and everything in between. If the purpose of a prologue is to prepare the reader for what is to come, taking time to breathe out therefore seems like good advice: for us, breathing out can be one way of entering into a vulnerable state, a momentary release of tension and making space for encounters with all the critters that are and are not ourselves; for strange futures yet to unfold; and for something unexpected to arrive.

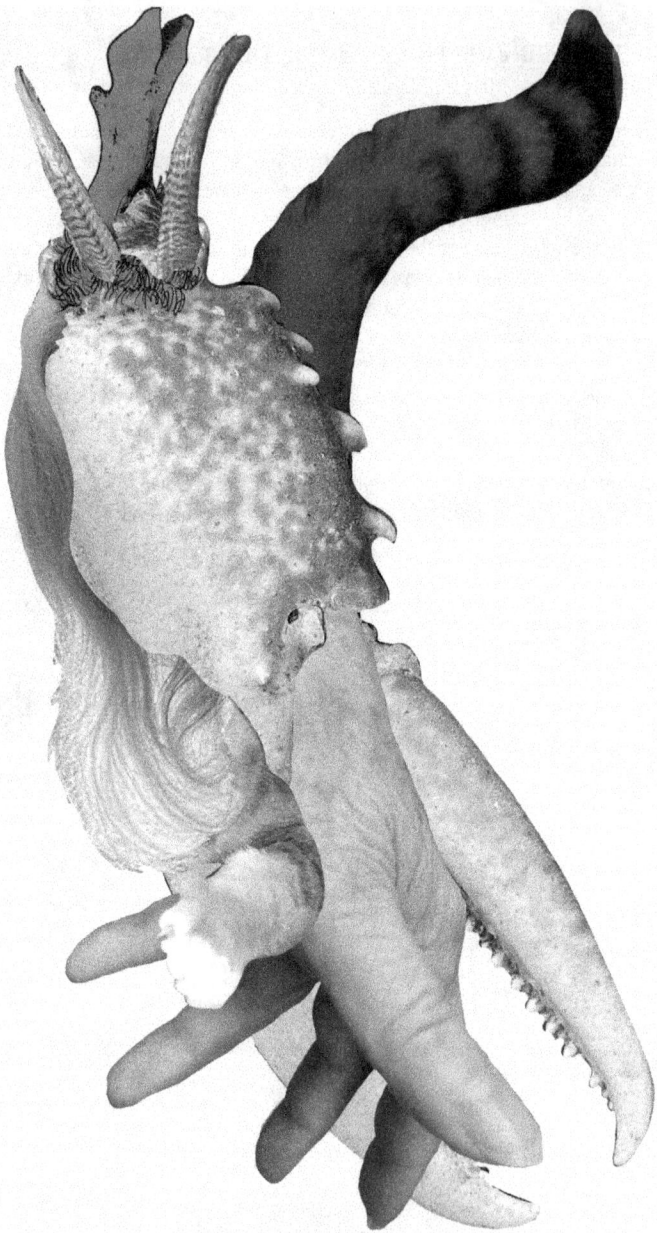

Figure 1.1 Alien Encounters – Estrangement. Collage created for this publication based on photographs by the three co-authors of this volume.

Source: © Katja Aglert 2023.

1 Reconfiguring Alien Encounters

Introduction

Nina Lykke, Katja Aglert,
and Line Henriksen

The tentacles were elastic. At her shout, some of them lengthened, stretching toward her. She imagined big, slowly writhing, dying night crawlers stretched along the sidewalk after a rain. She imagined small, tentacled sea slugs – nudibranchs – grown impossibly to human size and shape, and, obscenely, sounding more like a human being than some humans. Yet she needed to hear him speak. Silent, he was utterly alien.

(Butler 1987, 12)

"Come closer and look". She did not want to be any closer to him. She had not known what held her back before. Now she was certain it was his alienness, his difference, his literal unearthliness. She found herself still unable to take even one more step towards him.

(Butler 1987, 11)

Are "aliens" scary, hostile, and threatening monsters, little green men from Mars, bent on conquest, murder, and rape? In the initial scene of the novel *Dawn* (Butler 1987), from which the above quotes stem, Black feminist science fiction writer Octavia Butler plays with the conventional sci-fi trope of the hostile alien encounter. However, she reclaims it from feminist, anti-racist and more-than-human perspectives. The non-human aliens (Oankali) of Butler's novel, one of whom approaches the human protagonist, the Black woman Lilith Iyapo, in this initial scene, turn out to be patient, gentle, non-hierarchically minded, and caring. *Dawn* is set in a spaceship, made of living material, to which the Oankali have rescued a group of humans (Lilith included) after the latter more or less have destroyed the conditions for life on Earth through an atomic war. The Oankali are a highly developed species, valuing non-violence and peaceful gene trade with other species. In this sense, the novel contrasts their habitus with the human predilection for hierarchy and conflict that it indicates as the reason for the utterly self-destructive act of atomic war. Moreover, the Oankali have superior skills in biological regeneration, genetic engineering, and medical enhancement of bodies. Among other things, they

DOI: 10.4324/9781003373766-1

have the ability to cure cancer and regenerate the radioactively polluted Earth. After the rescue, the Oankali have put the humans to sleep for hundreds of years in order to have time to restore Earth to a liveable place before reviving them. The Oankali plan is to bring some humans (Lilith included) back home to Earth, hoping that they will accept to become a partner-species for the Oankali and interbreed with them. As the novel unfolds, Lilith becomes torn; on the one hand, she longs for human company and for a return to Earth. On the other hand, she becomes more and more attracted to the Oankali and their modes of collective living, based on a gently caring mutuality, a break with gender binarity, and empathic and egalitarian values. However, Lilith's first encounter with the asexual Oankali man, Jdahya, after her awakening from 250 years of sleep, is highly traumatic and governed by abjection (Kristeva 1982). Jdahya is gentle, patient, and empathic, but his non-human looks, in particular his tentacular sense organs, which look like oversized, writhing worms or sea slugs, produce an overwhelming phobic fear and visceral feelings of disgust in Lilith. However, as the encounter unfolds, she eventually comes to understand that her extremely negative response to Jdahya's alienness is prompted by his looks and not in any way by his actual behaviour.

We start this introductory chapter with quotes from the initial alien encounter in *Dawn*, because the book and Butler's *Xenogenesis Trilogy* (1987–1989)[1] to which it belongs, provide a strong feminist, anti-racist reconfiguration of this trope. Moreover, these sci-fi novels also align themselves forcefully with critical, more-than-human thought, even though the posthuman turn had not announced itself at the time of their publication. In much conventional science fiction, the alien encounter is modelled over colonial relations, ranging from "triumphal phantasies" of white explorers' appropriating alien "land, power, sex, and treasure" to "nightmarish reversals of the position of colonizer and colonized", when technologically superior aliens from Mars or other places in outer space come to invade and colonize planet Earth (Rieder 2008, 20).[2] By contrast to the conventional sci-fi repetition of violent and exploitative relations between colonizer and colonized, projected onto an encounter between humans and non-human aliens, Butler portrays the alien encounter as a revitalizing exchange, based on egalitarian and mutually benefitting engagements in xenogenetic (cross-species) interbreeding. Her novels and stories twist the sci-fi genre in order to critically expose its intertwinement with colonialist discourses on traveling to exotic places, motivated by desires for conquest, extraction, and exploitation. But her reconfigurations of the genre also shift the perspective affirmatively, opening possibilities for an envisioning of radically different, mutually enriching, caring, and non-exploitative worlding practices built on more-than-human companionships across species, bodily, and territorial borders. As noted by Black feminist and posthumanist scholar Zakiyyah Iman Jackson, Butler engages in a twofold ethico-political reclaiming of the conventional sci-fi trope. The non-human characters can be read metaphorically in relation to intra-human histories of colonialism and enslavement (2020, 130). However, according to Jackson, novels such as those in Butler's *Xenogenesis Trilogy* are also envisioning totally altered cross-species relations:

> Xenogenesis is defined as the production of offspring that are entirely and permanently unlike either parent. It is a form of (re)production that produces offspring that fail to reproduce the parents. In other words, xenogenesis is novel speciation rather than genetic variation within a species.
>
> (2020, 155)

Framing this book's investigation of ethical co-existence in more-than-human worlds with the figuration of the alien encounter and the figure of the alien as lens, we draw inspiration from the ways in which feminist, anti-racist, and posthumanist science fiction such as that of Butler reclaims this figuration. We are inspired by the use of the alien encounter and the figure of the alien as critical lenses to dismantle and denaturalize existing power structures as well as to articulate visions about alternative, egalitarian co-existence in more-than-human worlds. We follow in the footsteps of this kind of critical science fiction when, in a speculatively fabulating mode (Haraway 2016), it posits transformative encounters with more-than-human others as platforms for critical estrangement from the idea of human sovereignty and exceptionalism. Focusing in this book on encounters with such "strange" critters as Vulgar slugs, micro-algae of the group diatoms, and familiars (spirit helpers) of witches, we also try to mobilize platforms that can create productive estrangement, defamiliarization, and alternative ways of approaching and imagining human/other-than-human relationships. We, too, hope that our accounts and analyses of strange encounters can contribute to current eco-ethical and eco-political work to critically transgress the violent necropolitical worlding practices of extractive, racialized, and post/colonial capitalism and affirmatively envision new spiritual-material engagements with the world's multiple vitalities, of which we are part. The aim of the book is to investigate alien encounters with slugs, diatoms, and familiars as exercizes in unlearning of human exceptionalism and undoing of claims to absolute sovereignty on Earth, and in committing to developing our skills in the practicing of response-able, planetary companionship for social and environmental justice-to-come.

In this introductory chapter, we lay the foundation for these reflections. Firstly, we discuss how defamiliarization and estrangement work in critical science fiction and reflect on the ways in which our claims to follow the lead of this genre give us access to these tools as entry points to unlearning of human exceptionalism and undoing of feelings of entitlement to ultimate sovereignty over the other-than-human world. Secondly, we introduce the three alien figures with whom we want to enter into conversation in the book; we make ourselves accountable for our relationships to these particular three figures – Vulgar slugs, the micro-algae diatoms, and the familiar of the witch – and explain why they came to appear as our interlocutors. Thirdly, we provide an outline of the book's composition, its mixed-genre style, which combines poetic and philosophical writing modes, and the creative and experimental methodologies that overall guide the crafting of the five chapters and three Intertexts (Alien Arrivals) that follow this introduction.

Alien Encounters as Platforms for Cognitive Estrangement

According to classic science fiction theorist Darko Suvin, critical, socially oriented science fiction works, first and foremost, through the literary techniques of estrangement and defamiliarization. Suvin proposed the term "narrative of estrangement" (1979, 20–21) to characterize the critical branch of the genre, linking it with the concept of cognitive estrangement. This concept was first coined by Russian formalist theory (Shklovsky 1990) and later politicized in socialist playwright Bertolt Brecht's theory of anti-capitalist and anti-fascist theatre (Brecht 1964, 192). Suvin explained the estrangement effect as a making a recognizable representation unfamiliar: "A representation that estranges is one which allows us to recognize its subject, but at the same time makes it seem unfamiliar" (Suvin 1979, 6). Feminist science fiction theory (Barr 1993, 10–11; Bryld and Lykke 2000, 40) and decolonial theory (Tlostanova 2023) have also argued for estrangement and defamiliarization as important critical tools for imagining and thinking about social change. But in so doing, they have also underscored the need to make the social critique embodied and contextually situated, and the genre of critical feminist science fiction is well suited to do so. Embodied and contextualized estrangement happens in sci-fi novels such as *Dawn*, when, in a fabulating and speculative story-telling mode, readers are invited into another world – a world which, on the one hand, is radically "discontinuous" from the oppressive one in which we currently live but which, on the other hand, allows us to imaginatively "return" to the realities of our here-and-now world and see its power structures and oppressions in ways which deuniversalize and denaturalize them (Barr 1993, 10–11). Butler, for example, confronts her readers with intersections of racism and speciesism, while the novel's way of situating these phenomena in a totally alien environment, the world of the Oankali, effectively undermines and dismantles them as Lilith's phobic projections, which *Dawn*'s sequence of events eventually helps her to unlearn and overcome.

However, when we claim estrangement and defamiliarization as tools in this book, we also note convergences between radical science fiction studies and the work of a group of environmental humanities researchers who recently have promoted the transposition of participatory research methodologies from critical social research with humans to more-than-human worlds (Bastian et al. 2017). In addition to taking lessons from critical science fiction studies, we have also been inspired by the work of this group. Therefore, we want to underline that it, too, evokes "cognitive estrangement" (2017, 27) as one of the important dimensions of its radical experiments in doing research *with* rather than *about* more-than-humans. In spite of this convergence, the research group on more-than-human participatory research does not claim genealogies to critical science fiction studies and to the tradition back to Brecht and Shklovsky. Still, when evoking cognitive estrangement, Bastian and her team of co-researchers make it pertinent to reflect upon these convergences.

Taking up the challenge of this kind of cross-cutting reflection, we, firstly, note that Bastian and team refer to defamiliarization, already when discussing the ways in which participatory methods in social research with humans prompt participants to step back "from familiar routines, forms of interaction, and power relationships in order to fundamentally question and rethink established interpretations of situations and strategies" (Bergold and Thomas 2012, 1; Bastian et al. 2017, 27). Secondly, we find it noteworthy that Bastian and team emphasize that defamiliarization in participatory research becomes much more intensified when tried out in more-than-human contexts; in their case, it involves researching together with assistant dogs, a flock of bees, an old forest, and a river. A keyword here is "disorientation" (Bastian et al. 2017, 28) – a disorientation which, albeit not automatically, can lead to reorientation, unlearning, and relearning. A beekeeper who participates in the research, for example, reports that the participatory approach taught her to think carefully about the ways in which her practices could be "sympathetic to the bee's needs" (Ibid.). In other cases, the disorientation leads to silences, and a kind of frustrated but also productive stuckness, which throws the human participants back into a questioning of the research framework per se. This happens, for example, when Bastian and team (2017, 28) start from questions of informed consent when dealing with a river and end up critically questioning the notion of the autonomous and decontextualized individual which lies behind this concept. This framework is clearly not making sense in relation to the river. Instead, the researchers speculate, the river seems to call for being considered in its specificity and in the context of the broader natural-cultural landscape of which it is part. The river is not water in the abstract. It is a specific river in a specific landscape. The river acts as interlocutor in the conversation with the human researchers through this kind of specifics. So this is what the researchers speculatively come to understand that they somehow have to engage with.

To come to this kind of open-ended conclusion is an important part of the research. According to Bastian and team (2017), a main principle of more-than-human research must be to accept disorientations and be open to the cognitive estrangement which they prompt and the radical and unexpected contemplations and changes they require.

Affective Estrangement: Encountering Slugs, Diatoms, and Familiars

So far, we have discussed cognitive estrangement. We have looked at the science fiction genre's exposing of spatial and temporal discontinuity between fictive and "real" worlds, allowing the fictive ones to act as twisted mirrors, apt for putting the problems of the here-and-now world on display. We have also compared notes between the effects of these discontinuities of the science fiction worlds and disorientations in participatory research, in particular when it involves more-than-humans. The kind of cognitive estrangement theorized by both science fiction theory and more-than-human participatory research have inspired this book's critical-affirmative investigations of more-than-human relationalities through the figuration of alien encounters. However, it is also to be noted that we do not only focus on cognition.

Another important aspect of our engagement in alien encounters with slugs, diatoms, and familiars concerns affectivity, affective estrangement, and the question of unfolding of alternative sensibilities and sense-abilities (abilities to sense, Treusch 2017). This is an additional reason for starting with the quotes from *Dawn*, which clearly call attention to deep affective levels of response. The quotes spell out that there is a divide between Lilith's corpo-affective abjection and her cognitive recognition of Jdahya's empathic and "human"-like way of speaking and caring about her. Articulating this divide, Butler asks how to overcome it. Though, she also makes it clear that this is not only a question of thinking differently but rather about learning to develop alternative sense-abilities. This involves a complex corpo-affective learning process, as Butler spells it out through Lilith's example – a process, in which the human subject becomes able to sense in different ways from the habitual and normative ones. Butler also pinpoints how the divide between corpo-affective abjection and cognitive recognition in itself produces an affective estrangement, a productive disorientation, which, indeed, may be a first step towards changed sense-abilities. The process of becoming corpo-affectively disoriented but eventually also attuned to the new kind of transcorporeal experiences and be prompted to unfold new sense-abilities takes place throughout the novel. In a bodily sense, Lilith becomes more and more able to be close and intimate with the Oankali. But already in the beginning of the novel, Lilith's stream of consciousness shows us how the contradictions she experiences in Jdahya's appearance disorient her while also enabling her to enter into a state of affective estrangement. She becomes estranged to her own feelings of disgust, and this opens possibilities to start reasoning about them. The first quote shows this complex mix of disorienting and enabling affective estrangement. Lilith starts to meta-reflect on her disgust, and she notes that Jdahya's tentacled speech is "obscenely, sounding more like a human being than some humans" (Butler 1987, 12), but that she – in spite of the visceral disgust which this "obscenity" calls forward in her – at the same time needs him to speak, because it makes him more human-like, while "silent, he was utterly alien" (Ibid.).

The questions of corpo-affectivity and unfolding of alternative sense-abilities are important in the context of this book. The three alien figures, slugs, diatoms, and the witches' familiars, whom we (the three humans) have invited to be our interlocutors, are all, in different ways, embodying a corpo-affectively disorienting alienness – an alienness that for an immediate (modern) human consideration most often are seen as unfamiliar and negative, if not right away disgusting.

Slugs are often linked to abjection, and Vulgar slugs are considered particularly disgusting, referred to as an "invasive alien species" by mass media but also by influential governmental organizations such as, for example, the European Environment Agency (2009), an EU agency responsible for offering analytical expertise on environmental issues. These kinds of organizations note that the "invasions" are caused by human activity moving animals around the globe. Nonetheless, their rhetoric still constructs Vulgar slugs and other species which, as a consequence of human activities, spread in territories where they are "alien", as evil antagonists that threaten to destroy good environments and relations. Under the telling title *Killer Slugs and Other Aliens – Europe's Biodiversity Is Disappearing at an Alarming Rate*, these "aliens" are linguistically constructed as "pest species", "vectors of disease", "major threats", etc. (European Environment Agency 2009).

Micro-algae, among them diatoms, are in similar ways cast as being "harmful". They are counted among what tellingly is called "harmful species" (Hallegraeff, Enevoldsen, and Zingone 2021, 1). This is, first of all, due to their role in so-called "harmful algal blooms" (referred to through the acronym "HABs") – that is, excessive growth of algae in surface waters, leading to oxygen depletion that cause fish- and plant death at deeper levels, amounting to the emergence of aquatic dead zones (see, for example, the National Oceanic and Atmospheric Administration 2022). Again, governmental and scientific documents on the today globally widespread HAB phenomena tend to mention human activity (among others, agricultural businesses' discharge of phosphates and nitrogen in coastal waters) as a prime mover. But the algae are rendered as complicit killers, and popular media coverage intensifies the smokescreens cast around the human culpability, when official and scientific discourses link "species" and "harm", constructing the algae as per se "harm"-generating. It is telling for the state of the art of the scientifically and officially underpinned "harm" rhetoric that a scientific journal with the name *Harmful Algae* has existed since 2002.

Finally, the familiars – they, too, are endowed with a mostly negative image in mainstream modern discourses due to their affiliation with witches. Historically, the witch hunts, which were orchestrated at the threshold of European modernity, institutionalized a view of witches as devilish evildoers to be violently eradicated together with their demonic helpers and accomplices, familiars in the shape of black cats, toads, imps, etc. In more recent decennia, witches have been declared "superstitious" and "ridiculous", while their familiars accordingly have been rendered as non-existent products of "irrational" minds and likewise met with ridicule. But the fear and disgust are also still lurking underneath. In Denmark, the home country of Line and Nina, it has, for example, until very recently been a celebrated custom to put a witch doll on top of the midsummer celebration bonfires.

So a shared feature of all our alien interlocutors is that they, in mainstream imaginaries, figure as phenomena, which are likely to call forward negative feelings such as hate, fear, and disgust in (modern) humans.

Alienation: (Un)doing the Abyss between "Us" and "Them"

Like critical science fiction and participatory research with more-than-humans, it is our aim to create a productive cognitive estrangement and disorientation through our engagement with slugs, diatoms, and familiars in this book. But we also aim to produce a generative affective estrangement when we summon these figures as key interlocutors. We invite the figures into the book to help us to unlearn human exceptionalism and contribute to the undoing of the enormous historical act of alienation, which we consider the modern institutionalization of a divide between the superior human and the non-human world of inferior others to be. Like the "disgusting" Oankali in Butler's novel, the "invasive" "killer" slugs, the "harmful" diatoms, and the "evil" familiars exemplify the enormity of this historic alienation as well as the immensity of the both cognitive and affective work needed to overcome it. We want, in particular, to stress how negative associations that stick to the three figures spell out how a bridging of the divide and an overcoming of the alienation, next to serious cognitive change, also must involve a very corpo-affectively concrete learning process that puts altered sensibilities and sense-abilities central. Because, as Butler's description of Lilith's reaction to the Oankali so brilliantly suggests, a bodily change of aesthesis (preparedness to sense in specific ways) can be even more difficult to accomplish than a cognitive one.

How big a task it is to undo this divide and overcome the alienation is also becoming clear when we consider philosopher Jacques Derrida's reflections on the part of it which concerns the hierarchical separation of Human and Animal as nothing less than an "an abyss" (2002, 2008). We extend these reflections to encompass not only animals proper but also diatoms and familiars. We claim Derrida's evocative characterization of the divide as an abyss. However, insofar as it is only the slugs who fit an inscription into Linnaeus' 18th-century taxonomic categorization of the animal kingdom, we twist the Derridean framework. So instead of an abyss only between Human and Animal, we will instead speak of one between Human and Other-than-Human. This will make it possible to extend the reflections on the abyss to include diatoms and familiars. Diatoms transgress the taxonomy of animal versus plant (Allen et al. 2011), while familiars boldly defy the modern ordering of the world in real and non-real phenomena. Derrida challenged the latter in his reflections on spectres (1994) but did not bring this kind of ephemeral creatures into his reflections on the Human/Animal abyss. Twisting the Derridean reflections on the abyss to address also human relations to diatoms and familiars is, indeed, widening the gap to be bridged and making the task of trying to do so even more difficult. However, for us the bottom line in this is that we consider slugs, diatoms, and familiars as apt for radically dismantling and challenging our habitualized, human exceptionalist thought and comfort zones on the Human side of the abyssal divide. Like the Oankali in Butler's novel and the bees, trees and river in the more-than-human participatory research experiment of Bastian and team, our three alien figures are, in more than one sense, highly "difficult" cases.

Firstly, they are "difficult" because the negative associations adhering to them make them very easily slip into the image of disgusting, inferior aliens, clearly separated from "us" (the Humans) through the abyss, which appears to "us" as sustained by philosophy as well as by common sense and bodily intuitions. However, in addition to appearing as aliens due to the burden of negative associations, which the slugs, diatoms, and familiars share with the Oankali, they are, secondly, also "difficult" cases, because they are non-communicable in a human sense. In this way, they are different from the Oankali, but here, we can compare them to the bees, trees, and river in the research of Bastian and team. While the assistant dogs that also took part in the participatory research experiments of Bastian and team made it more easy for the researchers to start thinking about mutuality and participation (2017, 23–25), the question of the abyss and the enormity of the task of bridging it became palpably clear when the experiments on more-than-human participation proceeded to the work with bees, trees, and river (2017, 28). In contrast to the assistant dogs, who were trained to communicate with humans, the bees, the trees, and the river produced even more serious disorientations. As the slugs, diatoms, and familiars, they were not communicable in a human sense. Or, to phrase it differently: we must assume that all these beings communicate through very different and, for us modern humans, unusual and unrecognizable channels; but, like the burden of negative associations, this unrecognizability contributes to their specific ways of appearing as alien to "us" (humans). Their unrecognizable communication channels mean that we (the humans) even more easily slip into our epistemologies of ignorance and alienation from the other-than-human world, counting arrogantly on our habitual beliefs in the existence of a hierarchical abyss between "us" and "them" instead of trying to engage in the difficult and disorienting process of listening, learning, and trying to develop new sense-abilities.

The Coming into Being of This Book

This book and the collective as well as individual, artistic, poetic, and spiritual-material practices, on which it is based, is a creative exercize and a philosophical reflection upon the cognitive and affective estrangements produced by encounters between three humans and slugs, diatoms, and familiars. It is important to stress here that the initial encounters were not planned but came unanticipated. Semantically, an encounter is associated with an event that happens unexpectedly – in contrast to a meeting, defined as something planned in advance. Our encounters with slugs, diatoms, and familiars were in this sense true – that is unplanned, not chosen – encounters. So when we above have argued that slugs, diatoms, and familiars figure prominently in this book due to their burdens of negative associations and a conventional image of incommunicability in a human sense, it must, at the same time, be noted that these contemplations on shared grounds between our individually experienced encounters stem from a joint retrospective reflection. The most important reason slugs, diatoms, and familiars figure in this book is unrelated to these reasonings on their shared characteristics. We (the humans) summoned slugs, diatoms, and familiars into this book, because they arrived totally unexpectedly in our lives in moments, when, in different ways, each of us were in vulnerable, disorienting, and traumatic situations which made us open to an "alien" encounter.

The stories about these unexpected encounters and the reflections upon them which together make up the book are articulated by the three humans in written human language. Such a written book is evidently a medium for a specific kind of human communication. Instead of writing a book about the encounters, the slugs might have responded to them in terms of leaving a trail of slime, the diatoms might have built a cliff, and the familiars might have baked a book in the oven, spicing it up with rosemary and thyme from their garden. We do not know and can only use our limited human imagination to guess. The writing of books like this one might seem too clumsy for slugs, diatoms, and familiars, given their perhaps more sophisticated skills in communicating about vital planetary companionships, kinship relations, and co-existence. Still, like Butler's character, Lilith, as well as like Bastian and team, we (the three human authors) try to do our best in terms of reflecting and acting in responseable ways to the experiences of disorientation as well as cognitive and affective estrangement which our encounters with slugs, diatoms, and familiars engendered – and writing a book seemed to us to be an enriching way to compare notes about the transformative estrangements that the encounters initiated for us and the planetary companionship relations they gave rise to.

The book is introduced by a prologue and this introductory chapter on what it implies to reconfigure alien encounters. It is organized so it first tells the stories of the ways in which our alien encounters came about, while the second part presents our retrospective reflections upon them. Through poetic and narrative texts, Chapters 2 through 4 account for the ways in which slugs, diatoms, and familiars arrived in the lives of the three humans in situations, characterized by vulnerability and disorientation. The chapters make it clear that the initial encounters for all of us had more existential dimensions than being mere academic pieces of research in the conventional sense of a researcher subject deciding to produce knowledge about an object. In Chapter 2, Katja tells the story of her highly traumatic meeting with slugs in her garden and accounts for the ways in which it gives rise to a long-term art project based on processual investigations of human–slug relationships. Chapter 3 presents Nina's story of her entering into a queer loving companionship with diatoms, who eventually are becoming a key part of her spiritual-material mourning practices, because they built the cliffs and seabed where Nina's beloved lesbian life partner's ashes are scattered. In Chapter 4, Line explores her processes of coming to writing and overcoming stuckness and writing anxiety with familiars as tricksterous helpers/editors. Three collectively written intertexts, titled "Alien Arrivals: Slugs", "Alien Arrivals: Diatoms", and "Alien Arrivals: Familiars", are interspersed between these chapters. Through these collective texts, we try to respectfully summon slugs, diatoms, and familiars as writing companions. In the two final chapters (5 and 6), we reflect upon the stories of the alien encounters, told in the three Alien Arrivals texts and Chapters 2 through 4. Chapter 5 on more-than-human ethics and poetics, written by Nina, reflects on ethical dimensions of the changed sensibilities and sense-abilities which, across differences, emerged out of all three stories, as well as on the posthuman poetics that we interpellated to articulate them. Chapter 6 is a conversation between Katja and Line, including an interview they made with Nina, on the more-than-human methodologies which we have summoned in the book. An epilogue wraps up what we (the three humans) ourselves learnt from our alien encounters and companionships with slugs, diatoms, and familiars and invites readers to perhaps engage seriously with their own "aliens". The overall narrative which we tell through the sequence of chapters and Alien Arrivals texts is all the way through unfolding in conversation with the book's visual dimension. Collages, specifically made by Katja (one of them in collaboration with the artist Oskar Aglert) for this book against the background of photos and drawings by all three authors, as well as photos of slugs and diatomite cliffs, taken by Nina and Katja, and a few other images (a photo by surrealist artist Claude Cahun, a painting by Pieter I. Bruegel, and a photo of an orchid with a bee shape) address the themes discussed in the poetic, narrative, or philosophical texts in a kaleidoscopic manner, which calls forth new reconfigurations.

When accounting for the crafting of this book, we neither can nor will deny that the texts are written by three humans – perhaps or perhaps not supported by writing companions in the shape of slugs, diatoms, and familiars, whatever that may mean. That said, it is, however, also important to note that our wish to be true to the existential character of the alien encounters as they first took place for us and the (at least for the humans) transformative experiments in co-becoming and alternative co-existence which they led to made it urgent for us (the human authors) to disrupt the conventionally objectifying academic writing formats. This is why we instead have produced a mixed-genre book, which combines automatic writing, poetry, visual art, and philosophical and cultural analysis. We believe that the mixing of genres can facilitate attempts to go beyond the conventional objectification of the other-than-human world and contribute to unfolding of alternative modes of relating. The genre-mixing allows us to not only theoretically analyse the cognitive and affective estranging, dis-, and reorienting dimensions of the alien encounters but also to articulate the ways in which they have deeply affected us. Through the mixing of a multiplicity of genres, we try to articulate how the encounters and the contemplations of them changed our sense-abilities and understandings of what it takes to commit to an ethics of planetary companionship and kinship.

In the mixing of genres, we take inspiration from what one of the co-authors elsewhere has called Poetic Posthumanities, a "growing interest in hybrids of artistic/poetic and scholarly research, currently unfurling both in the artworld and at the critically posthumanist fringes of Academia that resist both neoliberal instrumentalization of research in hyper-utilitarian contexts, and nostalgic attempts to keep up the disciplinary borders of classic 20th century humanities" (Lykke Forthcoming b). Moreover, we draw on postqualitative methodologies which rely on the entanglement of creative/poetic/artistic and theoretical/philosophical insights as well as on more intuitively guided knowledge-shaping processes (St. Pierre 2018; MacLure 2021; Lykke 2022). This means that we emphasize that the poetic/artistic ways of shaping knowledge and the philosophical/theoretical ones are equally weighted. One is not a mere prosthesis for the other. Our poetic, visual, and story-telling formats are not to be understood as mere illustrations. In contrast, we see the poetic/artistic/narrative working modes and the philosophical/theoretical ones as intertwined in a non-hierarchical way. The poetic/artistic/narrative knowledge creation is important for the diving into intuitions, feelings, sensibilities, and corpo-affectivities and for articulating of poetic truths (Lykke 2010; Leavy 2016). The philosophical/theoretical knowledge shaping is important for the linking of thoughts and concepts in unexpected ways and for the unfurling of intellectually plausible and sustainable arguments. In our book, both these working modes are decisively important and demonstrate French philosophers Gilles Deleuze and Felix Guattari's point that thinking, feeling, sensing, and corpo-affective grounding are inextricably linked (Deleuze and Guattari 1994).

A Collective Writing Experiment

In terms of our work with different writing styles and formats, we shall in particular foreground that the book started from a collective writing experiment based on our inspirations from speculative fabulation (Haraway 2016) as well as from the method of automatic writing. Speculative fabulation refers to a wide range of narrative fiction, poetic, and artistic articulations that employ "fantastic", supernatural, spiritual, or other non-mimetic elements. As part of the unfolding of Poetic Posthumanities (Lykke Forthcoming b), speculative fabulation has gained momentum as a pathway to the reimagining of futures beyond the human-centred narratives of the Anthropocene.[3] Automatic writing is a poetic, artistic, and spiritual method. It emerged from spiritual practices (Conley 2016) and, in the decades after WWI, it also became intensely explored by writers and visual artists of the surrealist movement (Breton 1971; Rosemont 1998). The purpose was to delve into "alien" – surreal – worlds, where well-known, conventional realities could be defamiliarized and disrupted and horizons towards other worlds and worlding practices opened.

The three Intertexts, Alien Arrivals, are outcomes of this first collective writing experiment, a two-day writing workshop, which we framed through the notion of alien encounters with slugs, diatoms, and familiars. Through the notion of "alien encounter", we wanted to make estrangement and defamiliarization a starting point for contemplations of encounters with slugs, diatoms, and familiars which each of us (the human authors) had had previously. Rather than taking a more conventional academic approach and, first and foremost, relying on pregiven scholarly (human-centred) knowledge about the "alien" figures, we aimed at exploring speculative multi-voiced, more-than-human fabulations, using automatic writing to practice a decentred writing from non-unitary, embodied positions of enunciation.

The writing exercizes of the workshop were based on material related to slugs, diatoms, and familiars, whom the three human authors tried to summon as writing companions while attempting also to expose and disrupt exceptionally human subject positions and make space for transformative writing modes. Each of the human co-authors brought material and prompts related to the specific "alien" figure with whom they had entered into a companionship through an earlier, initial encounter and took turns in terms of leading a collective writing exercize, using these materials and prompts to help with the summoning of the other-than-human figures. The writing exercizes were carried out as automatic writing

As explored by writers and visual artists of the surrealist movement in the post-WWI period, automatic writing was inspired by psychoanalysis, but, as underlined by the author of the movement's first manifesto, French writer André Breton (1971, 298), should not be collapsed with stream of consciousness, a literary technique in modernist literature of the time. Stream of consciousness is commonly understood as an inner monologue, articulating literary characters as more-than-conscious subjects in a psychoanalytic sense, which disrupts boundaries between a rationally acting "I" and its unconscious bodily agencies. Automatic writing, however, breaks even more decisively with classical notions of the sovereign subject, reality, objectivity, and rationality than psychoanalysis does. As explored by the surrealists, automatic writing is a method for disrupting borders not only *within* the subject between conscious and unconscious dimensions but also *between* "I" and the world "out there", between subject and object, as ontologically separated entities. In the first *Surrealist Manifesto* from 1924, Breton famously defines surrealism as fundamentally challenging the borders between dream and reality: "I believe in the future resolution of these two states, dream and reality, which are seemingly so contradictory, into a kind of absolute reality, a *surreality*" (Breton 1971, 14). In its attack on "realism" in literature and art, surrealism and its arts practices (automatic writing included) is much more than psychoanalysis, implying a radical break with the reality principle of positivist ontology. This is a break which somehow brings surrealist thought and practice in resonance with more contemporary critiques of positivism, emerging among others from new feminist and posthumanist materialist philosophies as well as from decolonizing moves to revitalize indigenous cosmologies, which take dreamworlds seriously as facilitating transcorporeal intra-actions beyond modern Western dichotomies such as nature/culture and human/non-human (Anzaldúa 2015; Black 2018; Schaeffer 2018).

As noted by feminist philosopher Francesca Ferrando in an article on feminist genealogies of the posthuman in arts (2016, 4), there are resonances between post-1970s feminist body-, bio- and ecoart, and surrealist foremothers from the first half of the 20th century. To underscore the point about close genealogical relations between surrealism, posthumanism, and feminism in art, Ferrando quotes feminist artist and writer Penelope Rosemont (1998), who, in her seminal volume on the overwhelming but until very recently rather overlooked presence of women in the surrealist movement, pinpoints a "radical ecological awareness" in surrealist thought (Rosemont 1998, LI), which resonates with contemporary critical, feminist posthumanism (Ferrando 2016, 4).

Links between surrealism and *écriture feminine*, writing in the feminine, which, as articulated among others by French writer Hélène Cixous (1991), was important for the unfolding of feminist sexual difference theory, should also be noted (Lie 2014), as well as the ways in which the surrealist method of automatic writing has been developed in creative writing (Lykke 2014) with the aim of connecting writing to affect, embodiment, and poetics. These links were sounding boards for our use of automatic writing to collectivize the encounters with slugs, diatoms, and familiars which each of the human authors had had prior to our collaboration on this book.

In our collective writing experiments, we summoned the three figures as prompts for automatic writing. At the initial workshop, we did writing sessions on each figure, led by the co-author who interpellated this particular figure, prompting the group to write while summoning the figure through a poem, a small story, an image, an artefact, etc., associated with it. The automatic writing was, along the road, also interrupted by new prompts, chosen collectively or by the co-author in charge. The series of writing exercizes led

Figure 1.2 I Extend My Arms, 1931–32, Claude Cahun.
Source: Courtesy of Jersey Heritage.

us to the collective intertexts of this book – the three Alien Arrivals texts – which explore a process of collective co-becoming with the three figures while entering into transcorporeal conversations, corpo-affectively trying to poetically attune to the figures rather than re-present them in a conventional scholarly sense. The procedure is based on the assumption that automatic writing and poetic/artistic articulations can establish metonymic relations, relations of touch and contiguity (Jakobson 1987; Lykke 2022). A metonymic writing differs from a representational one, claiming to know the essential truth about what is represented. The aim is to substitute the traditional representational approach of science with a precarious search for vulnerable intimacy and kinship through poetic touching, that is, in a respectful way, reaching bodily out to the figures through poetic language rather than looking at alien others as if they were objects in need of representation.

As it is articulated in many ways in the Alien Arrivals texts, we do not believe that we can, just like that, shed our human skin and transgress our habitualized ways of approaching and interpreting other-than-humans. It is important to keep in mind that posthumanism "in its attempt to decentre the human, . . . is still thought and theorized by humans, in a human-centric system of signs" (Ferrando 2016, 4). As noted also by Breton (1971, 298), a human can only "in all humility, use the little he (!) knows about himself to reconnoiter what surrounds him". But according to Breton, and we follow him here, an effective way to do this is to go through "poetic intuition" (1971, 298), and "automatic writing" implies that this intuition is used in a "rawer" format than when it is filtered through more structured processes of chrono/logically ordered thought. So, in all modesty, collectively reaching out, trying to summon and get in touch with our figures through poetic intuition in the format of collective automatic writing experiments is what the Alien Arrivals texts are trying to do.

Notes

1 Octavia Butler's *Xenogenesis Trilogy* consists of the novels *Dawn* (1987), *Adulthood Rites* (1988), and *Imago* (1989). The trilogy was later published as a collection under the main title *Lilith's Brood* (2000).
2 An example is H.G. Wells's novel *War of the Worlds* (1898), filmed by Steven Spielberg (2005).
3 The Anthropocene, the Age of Anthropos (ancient Greek word for human being/man), figures prominently in current debates on the climate crisis, and the ecological crises more generally, which have raised questions about a geo-historical shift which implies that the planet is considered to have entered into a phase where human transformation of it is having decisive, permanent, and all-encompassing geological effects. There is still no official consensus among geologists about the shift and the concept. However, since a committee under the scientifically agenda-setting Geological Society of London in 2008 decided that a suggestion to use the Anthropocene-concept about the new geological epoch that Earth seems to have entered should be more closely investigated, the concept has come to take up a more and more central place in global debates on the human-induced ecological crises, which haunt the planet. Feminist, posthumanist, Black, and decolonial voices (Crist 2013; Haraway 2016; Tsing et al. 2017; Neimanis 2017; Yusoff 2018; Lykke 2019b) have contributed forcefully to the debate, foregrounding the necessity to radically rethink and practically reorient human/more-than-human relations, as well as criticized the notion of Anthropocene for its way of keeping up a humanocentric perspective.

Intertext I

Alien Arrivals

Slugs

Katja Aglert

The automatic writing for "Alien Arrivals: Slugs" was prepared by Katja through a prompt where she invited the human co-authors to go out into the garden behind Nina's house. There, she asked everyone to sit down on the ground. She handed out earplugs to silence the hearing and invited everyone to close their eyes. Then she gently sprinkled water on everyone's arms. A moment followed of sitting like this on the ground for a while, observing, feeling, and sensing. The idea was to imagine slug difference through multi-sensorial experiences, the specifics of this writing prompt being inspired by the fact that slugs don't have hearing or see very well but rather perceive their surroundings mainly through smell, taste, and touch.

Listening as a Touch Between Skin and Air, and Seeing as Tasting with all its Tentacles

1.

My arm sprinkled with moist,
not turning into a slug,
but embodying difference, and similarity.
Moist, moist, moist.
Moist like grass where sliding bodies move,
slippery like stones after rain,
slippery like slugs passing a footpath.
The water in my body,
through the pores of my skin,
leaking.
Moist, a life saver,
no moist no life.

DOI: 10.4324/9781003373766-2

2.

Silence, silence, silence.
Don't have ears.
Muffled world,
the humidity on my arm suddenly felt more intense.
The vibrations of drips
of moist rain on the body.
The sensation of gravel that are slided past,
or perhaps over.
Get stuck on sticky slug sole.

3.

What if slugs,
similar to algae,
turn into the next stage after this life?
Perhaps the sticky goo on slugs' tails are actually the slugs' familiar?
What goes on between life and death?
Deaf? Death?
A hearing aid, a sound proof world, a muffled noise, shouting wind,
silence, presence, the sound of computer keyboards, of hungry stomachs.
Hungry slugs eating,
each other if necessary,
embodying slugs, becoming death, fuelling life, turning moist into sticky
goo, attached to tail,
re-cycling, turning liquid into static,
water to ice,
algae to rock,
slug to figurine.

4.

I am not trying to understand,
only to get closer to becoming with.
To feel, to care, to expand what I am so far,
to speed up,
to slow down.
To notice difference,
to acknowledge what I might otherwise take for granted.
Bla bli blubbi blubb and sliiiiding silently over slimy surfaces,
in rain.

/K

Tales of people shedding their skin, donning the skin of others. Could I do that? Shed my skin, become a slug? No, not become a slug but become with a slug, borrowing its skin? What would the ritual for this exchange be? Would I have to give you my skin in return, slug? What would you do, then, a day in my skin? Or can we only do this at night, by the ghostly sheen of the moon? Donning my skin, walking the streets at night, where would you go, slug? Would you look after my skin? I have so many lotions, some of them acid, I don't think they would be good for you. As I slide on my belly, shedding your precious slime, I wonder what you're doing in the meanwhile. Do you pull my skin across the asphalt, forgetting about the two legs? My belly is bad for moving, I'm afraid, but then again, my feet are not the best either. I don't have much slime, this skin is very dry, it has very little to share with the ground, no trail to make that you may follow back out through suburbia, through the woods, the mountains. While moving slowly across a leaf, I start to wonder; maybe, with such dry skin, you'll have to open a vein and leave a trail of blood instead. Though not slimy, it'll be a trail, at least, something to follow.

I can't hear you. No footsteps. No heavy breathing as you climb the stairs. I set out to look for you but only see dense green grass. I call out, and the sound is so loud, it reverberates in my head. Church bells chime (ring ding ling), they announce the magic hour for the swapping of skin. There you are. We pull on our hides, and dawn breaks. I look down, and you look ahead, already on to new adventures. I move, unsteady, wondering where you've been, where I've been. I almost throw myself down on the stairs, wanting to move on my belly all the way up. Each step makes me dizzy, such speed, it's too quick! And so much noise – the creaking stairs, shouting in the distance, the barking of a dog. I open a door, and the hinges shriek, they hurt my ears, and all is so dry. I panic. I pull myself into the living room, feeling lost. There are scratches on my arms, and I open them and leave little smears of blood from one end of the sofa to the other. I curl up in the corner, a little more calm. I reach out for the remote and turn on the news, and there I am again, my face in the TV. I hear the newsreader say I crashed a car last night and walked through private woods.

I wake to the sound of church bells (ring ding ring dong) in the morning, maybe the night, I'm not sure. Time makes no sense any longer. I feel the wet in my arms, I feel sound in my ears. I try out my legs, and they seem to work. I move through the house and down the stairs. You are there again. I pull off my skin and give it to you, and I slip into your slime, and it is cool and comforting. We'll be all right, I think. Now I can always find my way, and I think you wanted to get lost. This we can give each other.

I can no longer hear the church bells. All is quiet and wet. I make my way across grass and dirt and into something I no longer have words for.

/L

Moist, moisture on the hand – a moist body is important when you are a slug. How to symphysize with a slug?

Imagining what makes pleasure for a slug?
How to have bodily empathy with a slug?

When does a slug feel really good? When it is raining – spring rain, summer rain, when it is hot in the air and wet all around. I am sure that would be a pleasurable situation for a slug. Slug, slimy, moist, loving moisture – symphysizing through love and pleasure, not love for slugs but rather feeling pleasure and love with slugs. A childhood memory awakes. Toddler-Me in the woods of Asserbo. The grown-ups suddenly absorbed elsewhere, finding chanterelles abounding all over the forest floor. The chanterelles love the wet, warm, rainy weather, too. Chanterelles everywhere. The grown-ups for a moment forgetting Toddler-Me. Suddenly, I am surrounded by snails, called forward by the warm, wet forest floor, full of mosses, grass, leaves. All grown-ups gone. No-one to save me from the snails, attacking me from everywhere – sneaking slowly in on me. I get so scared – I cry out loud. Nightmare-vision: snails coming towards me from all over. Standing there in the middle of the forest, everything around me, green, rainy, warm, wet, and then all these snails encircling me. Snail pleasure – green, rainy, warm, wet snail pleasure. Intensely dripping trees; grass, leaves, mosses, everything so green, intensely green. I cannot escape. The circle of snails is unbreakable. Spellbound, surrounded, totally stiff, I just stand there – and cry, cry, cry out loud. My mother runs towards me – what is happening? She lifts me out of the circle of snails – hugs me, explains that snails are not dangerous. I don't believe her. They are dangerous. Very dangerous, indeed. They'll suck me up, swallow me. I would not exist by now had my mother not rescued me from the snails' magic death circle. Why did Toddler-Me become so panic-stricken? What kind of upbringing makes modern toddlers believe that snails enjoying themselves in the wet grass are out to kill them? What makes certain animals abjectable to modern humans?

How to symphysize with a slug?

/N

2 Encountering Vulgar Slugs

What Can a Bite Tell about More-than-Human Becomings?

Katja Aglert

Invitation to a Slug

Dear Slug,

Squatting by the side of the pavement, moist after rain, I stretch out my index finger towards you in an attempt to invite you to join me as a companion in the writing of this chapter. My legs are quickly going numb, you take your tttiiimmmeee sliding towards me, releasing behind you a silver trace of slime. Your tentacles touch the tip of my finger, and then your teeth, followed by a sensation of what I can only understand as you chewing on me. Tasting me. Is this the beginning of our writing companionship? Would you like to taste the drafts I am typing? Metabolizing them through your body into new material for continuous process? Until further notice, I will just try and stay here, paying attention to the feeling of a wild slug chewing.

Yours faithfully,
Katja.

*

While slime can certainly be disgusting, it hadn't occurred to me that it might be interesting.

(Bailey 2010, 70)

*

Uninvited Dinner Guests

Tentacles at the doorstep stretch towards me as I open the front door with one hand, a glass of beer in the other, about to walk out into the garden to sit down and enjoy the last rays of sun at dusk. The tentacles are attached to a ten-centimeter oblong, brown, slimy body now on its way over the doorstep towards our hallway. I realize that I should probably do something. I put the beer down and grab a pair of garden gloves with a red flower pattern. I squat

DOI: 10.4324/9781003373766-3

and pick up the creature with my glove-coated fingertips. The tentacles immediately disappear into the slimy body (how is that even possible?). Despite the fact that my skin is not in direct contact with the body, I sense a dense rubber-like mass underneath my fingertips. The very thought of having to touch such a body without protection is unimaginable. I observe that the body has now transformed into a little curved ball, presumably for protection, and realize that this is a mutually disturbing encounter. The bodily reaction reminds me of the posture called "Duck and Cover" from a TV commercial with the same name from the 1950s. I believe it was produced in the US during the Cold War in order to teach the public how to act if exposed to a nuclear bomb. In the commercial "Duck and Cover" is cheerfully sung, while numerous people show the viewer how to take cover and curl into the shape of a ball in their homes and on the streets. As if that would make a difference. I walk to the edge of our garden and throw the slimy body as far away as I can, across the border of our land. I walk back feeling pleased with myself, thinking that the beer is now even more well deserved. The moment I sit down in the garden, I discover another slimy creature with tentacles, this time sliding up onto the house facade. With a shiver, I wonder if these slimy aliens have some kind of unpleasant agenda, yet unknown to humans.

Around the same time as this event took place, a motion was presented in the Swedish government that proposed to develop an action plan for how to combat the Vulgar slug[1] (*Arion vulgaris*) (Rowson et al. 2014). The slug, nicknamed *Mördarsnigeln*[2] (translated from Swedish as "the killer slug"), is conceived as a harmful alien invasive species.[3] In this motion it was described how not only private gardens were affected by the slug's taste for plants but, above all, how commercial vegetable farms were exposed as well. One farmer informed that they killed 55,000 slugs during the summer of 2007. This particular summer was described as the one with the highest number of Vulgar slugs in Sweden. Denmark was put forward as a guiding example for how to handle the situation with increasing numbers of Vulgar slugs by funding research and collecting data about the slugs' behaviour and, from this information, develop strategies for how to hold back the invader's rampage. This summer in 2007, when Vulgar slugs were headline news in Swedish media, was the time when I encountered this, to me, alien creature for the first time. Encountering the creature in the garden of the little country house that we had managed to buy, I at first mistakenly thought the brown thing on the grass was cat poop and cursed our neighbour's cats for using our lawn as a toilet. After further examination, I realized that this was not the case. Simultaneously, I discovered more and more slugs in our garden, eating delicate leaves of the potted basil, sliding onto the freshly plastered facades, gathering under bushes in what, to me, looked like wild orgies, or stretching out on the grass (as if owning the place).

As long as I can remember, I have considered myself to be someone who cares for animals. All of a sudden, in the context of my country-house garden,

I found myself thinking about the most efficient ways to exterminate a population of slugs that seemingly, from my viewpoint, intended to take over our garden. As if speaking from the isolated space of a nation state, I noticed military rhetoric unfolding in my mind: the right to strike back if attacked by an enemy. I observed how this thinking prompted me to justify my preferred choice of method for extermination, which was beer traps. We installed several of them in the garden. The idea and function of beer traps are based on the Vulgar slugs' fondness for beer. With their excellent sense of smell, they are attracted by the beer smell and slide towards the beer-filled bucket. The bucket is usually placed in a hole in the ground, leaving the bucket edge at the same level as the ground, making it easy for the slugs to get in. They slide down into the beer trap and start to drink and gradually become drunk. Thus, they are not able to slide back up to safety but instead glide downwards and drown in the liquid. The reality of this is a dreadful scene. They turn and twist in the liquid for quite some time before they slowly suffocate. When in distress, slugs release slime,[4] which mixes with the beer, gradually turning the liquid into a mix of dead slugs, beer, and slime. Despite this, new slugs arrive in the beer trap and drink, most of them eventually joining the mixture, while a few of them somehow stop drinking before it's too late, return to safety on land, and move on with their lives. When in our garden and looking down into the bucket with hundreds of dead bodies floating, I was torn between my care for animals and a fear of aliens.

In an attempt to understand more about the alien encounters in our garden, I decided to start documenting these events with my video camera. By zooming in with my camera lens, I made it possible to come closer to the slugs. In this microcosmos, the details of their elongated bodies resemble mountain ranges running in parallel, creating vast topographies shaped by repeated formations. The Vulgar slug's mantle and head look very different up close, like soft desert rock smoothened by sand and wind. When the slug moves, every part – the sole, tentacles, head, skirt, foot, mantle, and more – seem to dance in synchronized movements together with their surroundings. The tentacles turn in all kinds of directions, feeling their way, while the tip of the tail (which often has a sticky lump that looks like dirt attached to it) rocks up and down in rhythmic connection with the movements of the slug. Vertically, sideways, upside down, the slug seems to be unstoppable, always finding ways to navigate over, around, and under whatever obstacle they encounter.

I edited the recorded video documentation of the slug–human events from that summer into the artwork *Momentary Seizures* (Aglert 2007). Through video and sound, it articulates a multi-layered story, which speaks from a situated human "I" contemplating the conflictual alien encounters between humans and slugs in a country-house garden. The work raises questions around issues such as "the indifference to the suffering of others, and how we naturally kill so-called 'lower creatures' because they happen to be in our way" (Curman and Zamora 2007; Translated from Swedish by author). The slug-human events were discussed in metaphorical terms, drawing on parallel events outside of the garden where the "connotations are horrible; war rhetoric, genocide and terror. But the worst is the realization that it is impossible to assure that this evil isn't in all of us, in every human, when we without hesitation practice biological cleaning in our gardens" (Ibid.). Despite its attempts to trouble the human-centred perspective, which would allow us to unproblematically exterminate so-called lower creatures, *Momentary Seizures* is articulated from an, at the time, unreflective, anthropocentric point of view in which little attention was paid to the specific agency of the slugs in the garden.

Later, as part of a collaboration in another project with sociologist, animal studies, and gender scholar Tora Holmberg, in a discussion about human–animal relations and the politics of place, she asked the question: who gets the privilege to claim the function of space (Holmberg 2013; Holmberg and Aglert 2017, 131)? This, applied to my own artistic process with exploring the alien encounters between humans and Vulgar slugs, became a relevant shift for me towards questioning the common understanding of "the world" based on human exceptionalism. As part of my continuous investigations,

Figure 2.1 Momentary Seizures, 2007, Katja Aglert. Still image from video art work with detail of drinking slug in a beer trap.

Source: ©Katja Aglert.

I asked myself what it could mean to refuse the deadly violence, which, up until that point, had been part of these alien encounters between me (the human) and Vulgar slugs. How could the anthropocentric perception of these alien encounters be challenged through artistic process and articulation? It became a question of thinking together with Donna Haraway in relation to her proposal for making kin in the Chthulucene, "learning to stay with the trouble of living and dying in response-ability on a damaged earth" (Haraway 2016, 2). *Momentary Seizures* became the starting point for a long-term and ongoing artistic investigative process, which seeks to reconfigure the ways that the alien encounters between slugs and humans are performed. To do so, the project asks what it might mean to take into consideration not only human agency but also slug agency as part of these worlding practices.

The Lunch Invitation

On one side of the narrow pavement, there is a row of houses with gardens. On the other side, there is a small road with a dense stream of cars and buses. Humans, dogs, bikes, gastropods, and insects cohabit this pavement, with the overwhelming traffic noise drowning out the sounds of the many birds that are chatting in the surrounding trees and bushes. The smells of lilac and dust fill our bodies. We are out on one of our daily lunch walks. My partner notices a little garden snail sliding on the sunny pavement, the snail track glittering in the sunlight. We stop and both squat to spend a moment zooming into the microcosmos of the snail. I am not sure how this idea came to me, but suddenly, I find myself placing my finger on the ground a couple of centimeters from the snail. We sit there, temporarily blocking the pavement; I with my index fingertip feeling the warm temperature of the asphalt, my partner filming the potentially unfolding events with his smartphone. With astonishment, we notice the snail change direction and that their attention is clearly turning towards my finger. The tentacles are waving as if they are detecting details in the air much more complex than what we, the two humans, can comprehend. The snail moves with what seems like determination towards my finger, comes close, and eventually touches my fingertip with one of their upper tentacles. It is a light touch with the round shape at the far end of the tentacle, the eyeball. The tentacle seems to react with surprise, as if it did not expect to bump into something, and quickly arches backwards. Next, the lower tentacles (which they smell with) examine the skin of my finger closely, and soon, the little snail's mouth is within reach of my finger. The mouth of a snail or slug contains "thousands of microscopic teeth, called a radula" (Vendetti n.d.) with which they scrape up food to be rasped. The gentle feeling of a wild snail's mouth on my finger, scraping the skin with their radula, is a feeling of sheer thrill, a pleasant sandpaper-like sensation, a bit like a cat's tongue. After a while, when my legs are aching from the unusually long time squatting, I carefully pull away my finger from the little snail, feeling excited about this alien encounter.

I asked the gastropod scientist Ted von Proschwitz[5] if the snail's interest in my finger can be explained scientifically, and he told me that the reason for the interest is most likely related to smell and temperature, which are the decisive senses when it comes to guiding the foraging of gastropods. Snails and slugs "have evolved to eat just about everything; they are herbivorous, carnivorous, omnivorous, and detritivorous (eating decaying waste from plants and other animals)" (Ibid.), and so they follow warm temperatures, as decaying organic matter emits heat. Thus, the small snail was likely drawn to my finger in their search for food. Knowing this, I have continued to "invite" individuals from the gastropod worlds to encounter me, as food or for other yet-unknown reasons, by placing my finger on the ground.

The reason I continue to invite "random gastropods" to encounter me by placing my finger on the ground is that I am interested in exploring what it might mean to support and nurture a deeper awareness of ethically responsible methods in relation to more-than-human participatory worldings as well as taking into consideration a more-than-human ethics of companionship (Lykke 2022, 184). These issues have surfaced against the background of my diverse artistic experiments for performance pieces outdoors, where I have tried out different forms of practices for inviting Vulgar slugs to participate together with me as part of the artistic explorations. Initially, the way I practiced this act of "inviting" was by collecting slugs and carrying them from the place where I found them to the site of the performance experiment.[6] When analyzing my artistic material in retrospect, as well as having learned more with and about slugs, I have come to realize that the practice of inviting by "collecting and placing" slugs at the performance scene resulted in exposure to stress for most of them. They stayed for a long time curved into protective balls, and after slowly unfolding, most of them showed signs of wanting to escape the performance scene, clearly not feeling invited. Consequently, in my continuous projects with Vulgar slugs, one of my key concerns has been to develop more ethically responsible methods. Building further on this, I have been inspired by the concept of *more-than-human participatory research* (MtH-PR) and its emphasis on process and invitation to experimentation with methods, which "might better support more sustainable ways of living together" (Bastian et al. 2017, 2) as well as "explore whether the injunctions of western anthropocentrism might have unnecessarily restricted how participation is imagined" (Bastian 2017, 19). Another point, which I find meaningful in relation to my artistic participatory explorations together with Vulgar slugs, is to ask what it might entail to put "ourselves in a position where we would be confronted with what it might mean to even *try* to include nonhumans in PR processes" (Bastian 2017, 20). In

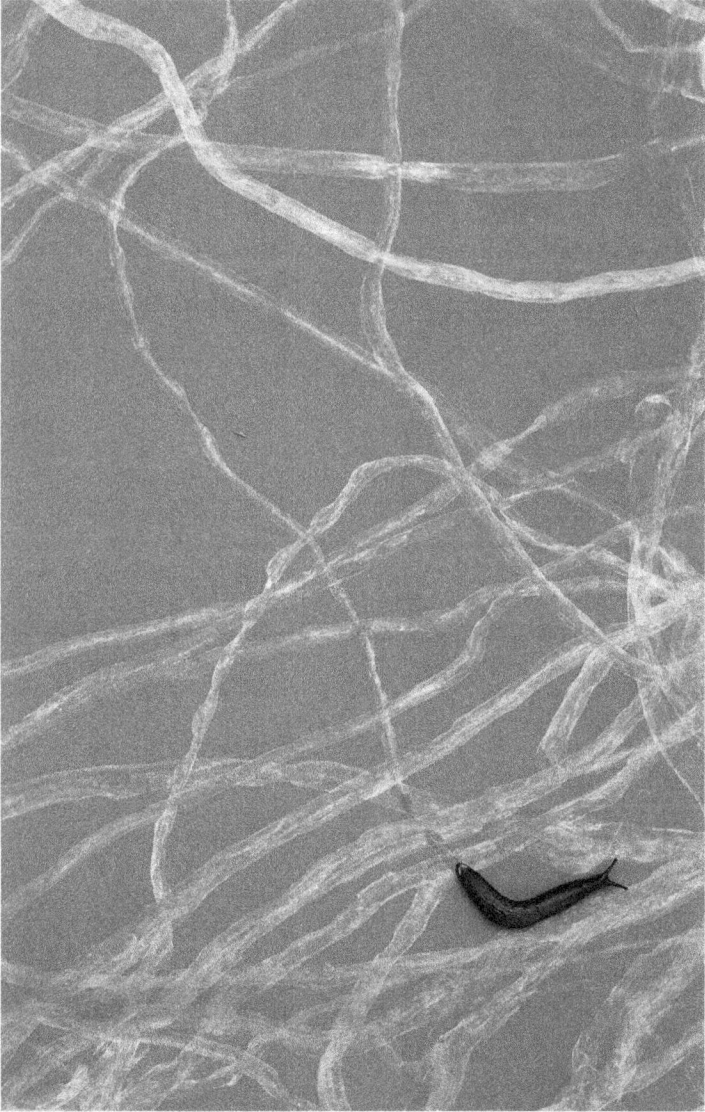

Figure 2.2 Turning Over the Grounds of sgulS, 2017, Katja Aglert. Documentation
detail of art performance with slugs.

Source: ©Katja Aglert.

this connection, I have searched for ways to invite Vulgar slugs to come and participate on their own terms. My finger invitations form part of this artistic process of learning through participatory research together with diverse gastropods. This has subsequently prompted me to challenge my own habits of pace through slowing down and positioning myself closer to the ground to make it possible for me to be more attentive to multi-sensorial modes of being. Slowing down has helped me realize that in order to invite gastropods to participate in anything, I have to depart from my own habitual ideas of how to perceive the world, which is mainly through vision and hearing. Instead, I have to include multiple sensorial perceptions, such as touch, smell, and taste, which are the main senses (Williams 2009, 55) for gastropods to interpret their surroundings.

Becoming Food

While expanding my interest from the specific Vulgar slug species towards a larger interest in gastropods, I acknowledge that this does not mean that I believe they are all the same (Pitt 2017, 92). This has not only become clear to me when reading biological facts about diverse species in the gastropod pluriverse (de la Cadena and Blaser 2018), but I have really felt their differences when I have spent time with them through diverse material multi-sensorial encounters. Especially during the numerous events when I have invited them to encounter me by placing my finger on the ground. One of these particular encounters prompted the question: can a slug bite be considered a co-writing activity prompted by a slug? This question came to me on the island Fur in Denmark in the summer of 2022, when I and Nina gathered in a house to write and spend time with our two alien figures: diatoms and slugs. The house we rented was situated at the top of cliffs rising high above the sea level and overlooked a magnificent view of the Limfjord land, sky, and waters. The same waters where the ashes of Nina's beloved life partner are spread.

Soon after our arrival, we stood in the grass behind the house and took in the view and felt the present moment with its variety of fragrances and cacophony of sounds. I felt the sunny breeze on my skin. A little later, around dinnertime, I discovered a large Vulgar slug in the grass. I squatted and observed the slug closely, struck by their surprisingly fast chewing of a leaf that had attracted their attention. Bite by bite, I saw the outline of their rows of teeth at the edge of the leaf and how the leaf disappeared into the slug's metabolizing bodily processes. I could hear the sound of the slug chewing, while at the same time, above us, a thunderstorm quickly approached. After a while, I turned back into the house to stay dry, as the slug remained in the same spot, presumably enjoying the waters pouring from the sky, supporting their life, which depends on staying moist.

The following day, the sky was clear and the garden humid and lush from all the rain, ideal conditions for snails and slugs to crawl out of their shells and shelters. I walked out to see if I could find any of our slimy friends and found a slug, which seemed to me to be the same individual that I observed chewing a leaf in the same spot the day before. That was not surprising since it is not uncommon for a slug to live their life in the same area. The rather large size of this individual was quite particular, which is another reason for my suspicion that it was the same one. Up until this point, I had never, as far as I know, encountered the same snail or slug twice. To encounter this slug a second time evoked a new feeling in me, perhaps a feeling of familiarity. I walked back into the house to get a cherry that, on my return, I dropped in the grass a couple of centimeters from my slimy companion. The slug immediately turned their tentacles in the direction of the cherry and approached with what seemed like resolution. After carefully investigating the potentially eatable thing, the slug eventually started to work on the cherry with their radula. When observing this activity, I was thinking to myself that I do not believe I have ever seen someone ssslllluuurrrpppiiinnnggg a cherry with such delight. When I returned to the same spot some time later, I noticed the cherry stone lying in the grass absolutely clean, nothing left to waste.

In my experience, it is common that when one spots a Vulgar slug in a garden, there are usually many more to be found. This did not seem to be the case in the garden in Fur, where I could not find any other slugs except for that large slug in the same spot, munching delicate leaves in the grass. In my excitement about the evolving relationship with this special slug, I repeated the act of visiting the "slug spot" in the garden the next day as well, where I yet again found our little companion. This time, Nina joined me, and we observed the slug with amazement. Soon enough, I extended an invitation to the slug by placing my index finger in the soft grass. As expected, the slug started to move towards my finger: tentacles, mouth, radula, sole, and the skirt swagging like the waves of the water in the fjord behind us. Nina pulled out her smartphone and started to film. Surprisingly fast, the slug moved up onto and along my index finger, covering my entire finger with its length. I turned my hand a little to guide the slug, so it would not crawl further up on my hand and arm, which I would not feel comfortable with. The slug instead turned towards the nail of my thumb. The sensorial experience of the slug's radula working on my skin and their sole moving on my finger was quite immersive. I felt animated by this alien encounter and sensed that this feeling was somehow shared by Nina as well as the slug, who both seemed absorbed by the encounter. We excitedly enjoyed the moment for what felt like quite a while. Suddenly and unexpectedly, I sensed an unpleasant feeling of pain, like a sting. Then another one.

Figure 2.3 Documentation image of one of the "finger invitations" between Katja and
a Vulgar slug on the island Fur, Denmark, 2022.

Source: ©Katja Aglert.

Much later, when I watch the video recording that Nina made with her phone, the film sequence shows the slug working on my finger while birds twitter in the extraordinarily beautiful surroundings, and Nina asks me:

– How does it feel?

After a moment, pulling myself out of the embodied experience of the alien encounter with a slug, I reply in a dreamy tone:

– It feels really fantastic.

Nina continues:

– In what way?

Then she adds in a whisper, almost as if thinking out loud to herself: So soft. I reply:

– It's a really strange feeling of softness that is extremely light. I can hardly feel it, but at the same time, I feel it very distinctly. Now, I can feel it a little bit more when the chewing is activated.
– So it's chewing now?
– Now, it is actually biting a bit hard. That's not ok.
– It's biting hard? So it's too much?
– Yes, it's too much, ah, you see, it's bleeding.
– Oh, wow!
– That's wild! So the slug was trying to eat me, literally.

Just like that, I plunged into the fleshy experience of myself actually being part of, in the ecofeminist philosopher Val Plumwood's words, "the animal order as food, as flesh [. . .] with being part of the feast and not just some sort of spectator of it, like a disembodied eye filming somebody else's feast" (Plumwood 2012, 15). The slug was eating me, tasting me, tearing off a piece of my cuticle as if it was a piece of lettuce. Except that this was flesh, a piece of my body. There was blood. As gently as I was able to in my unpleasant situation, I turned my finger at an angle so that the slug had to let go of it and stood up and left slug land to clean the wound on my finger with antiseptic.

The wound on my finger has now healed. However, parts of the wound remain in a still transformative mode in the sense that I still process the experience on different levels. This transformative mode could be approached through the work of Bayo Akomolafe, who proposes that "[s]ome wounds are portals to our rhizome universes of other ways of being and becoming" (Akomolafe 2021). My slug wound became a portal to an initial crisis, which was felt through fear and unpleasant surprise and which prompted new considerations for human–slug co-becomings. The crisis caused by the wound became a portal, which guided me into other ways of being and becoming.

As part of my reflections on what "other ways of being and becoming" might mean in relation to the slug wound, I would like to share some notes based on an interview[7] that Nina made with me the day after the slug bite, in which she initially asked me to describe my feelings. I replied to her that I was concerned by the fact that I had been bitten by a wild, omnivorous animal and that I "wasn't sure what was going on with the bacteria in their mouth and how that eventually would affect me". The situation made me very anxious, as it evoked a fear for my own health through the risk of getting infected with tetanus. This, in turn, invoked an abject feeling for Vulgar slugs, which was unexpected since I thought I had gotten over that through my many years of learning together with and about them through the artistic explorations and other research. In tandem with these feelings, I describe to Nina that I felt unpleasantly surprised about the fact that the slug would bite me: "How could you bite *me*, I'm on your side. . . . I was struck . . . by the fact, the realisation . . . I am not dealing with someone the same as myself". My comment resonates (without any other comparison) with the ideas that Val Plumwood discusses in connection with her experience of "becoming food" in a crocodile attack, which she miraculously survived. She describes that in the moment when she was "grabbed by those powerful jaws" (Plumwood 2012, 11), she sensed that there was something ultimately wrong and "*some sort of mistaken identity*" (Ibid., 12) at play. She continues: "This creature was breaking the rules, was totally mistaken, utterly wrong to think I could be reduced to food. As a human being, I was so *much more than food*. It was a denial of, an insult to all I was, to reduce me to food" (Ibid., 12). What Plumwood helped me see in relation to my own experience of becoming food for a slug was my idea about myself as a human. Among many things, I realized that I was, and still am, stuck in the Western culture of denial "that we humans can be positioned in the food chain in the same way as other animals" (Ibid., 16).

Let us return to the question which was prompted by the slug-finger event on Fur: can a slug bite be considered a co-writing activity, prompted by a slug? As I see it, the bite became the transformative mode, which propelled the artistic process and the writing of this chapter. I suggest that the slug bite pushed me out of the assumption that I, with my "finger invitations", was practicing something other than human exceptionalism. It was not until I was wounded, until I became food, that I came closer to something which could be understood as taking into consideration slug agency. The wound pushed me out of human control into fear, which showed an example of what it might mean – thinking together with MtH-PR – to even *try* (Bastian 2017, 20) to invite a slug to do participatory research. On the other hand, as suggested by Nina in our post–slug-bite conversations,[8] the fear caused by the bite wound pushed me *out of* research mode into bodily negative affect beyond the idea of Western human rationality. This research was also a mode, which assumed that experiences of slug-human encounters are always "positive" or pleasant (for the human). Thus, the wound became a portal for me to learn other ways of becoming with slugs through negative affect, beyond the rationality of (participatory) research, "without guarantees or the expectation of harmony with those who are not oneself – and not safely other either" (Haraway 2016, 98). Furthermore, in tandem with Amaya Schaeffer's discussion on Gloria Anzaldúa's practice of *communing-with* through their feminist and queer methodology in *Borderlands/La Frontera*, I propose that the slug bite can be considered an invitation to "a practice that entails a willingness to make oneself vulnerable to other embodiments of visioning and to surrender the safety of rational thinking and progressive time" (Schaeffer 2018, 1007). In this sense, the bite could be understood as an opening up of a new space for cultivating response-ability (Haraway 2016, 68) through more-than-human affective multi-sensorial modes of learning. I contemplate this as I imagine the piece of my flesh, the cuticle, inside the slug body, becoming part of their metabolizing process. Eventually, my flesh will turn to slug excrement, which will exit the slug body and seep down into the grounds of Fur, fertilizing continuous lively archipelagic relations (Glissant 2012, 41).

Hors d'Oeuvres

In this chapter, I have discussed what it can mean to invite a Vulgar slug to become a writing companion. However, a deeply foundational part of the making of the chapter as well as the book has also been the invitations we – the human writing companions of this book, that is, myself, Line, and Nina – have extended to each other as well as to our respective alien figures through the method of automatic writing. These collaborative automatic writing sessions and the conversations related to them have resulted in the Alien Arrivals Intertexts included in this book but have also been formative for the process of our book as a whole. In what follows, I put this chapter into conversation with some aspects of the "Alien Arrivals: Slugs" text.

In the "Alien Arrivals: Slugs" text, Line examines what it might mean to "become with a slug" through the idea of human and slug exchanging skin. The consequences of this act, as imagined by Line, become a tale in which that which is normally taken for granted in a "human sense" is shaken. She articulates the crossing of (human) boundaries and comfort zones through bodily, sensorial dimensions – for example, relating to speed and sound – which, for a slug, in comparison to a human, are very different, much slower, and mute: "I almost throw myself down on the stairs, wanting to move on my belly all the way up. Each step makes me dizzy, such speed, it's too quick! And so much noise – the creaking stairs, shouting in the distance, the barking of a dog" (Ibid.). Though, to me, Line pushes the boundaries of (human) comfort even further in the parts of the story where the protagonist "I", in the transformative state between the exchanging of skins, seems to gradually be absorbed into a liminal space, which troubles a clear separation between the human and the slug: "I pull off my skin and give it to you, and I slip into your slime, and it is cool and comforting" (Ibid.). To me, this seems to materialize a disruption of the idea of human exceptionalism, a queering of the presumed static boundaries between that of the so-called human and animal. At the end of her story, Line emphasizes this even further by moving the protagonist beyond language "into something I no longer have words for" (Ibid.). To me, Line's story articulates a vibrant case for the role of imagination in explorations related to more-than-human storytelling and is something which reverberates with the process through which we have developed this project and book, which has been central to my artistic explorations discussed in this chapter.

From another perspective in the "Alien Arrivals: Slugs" text, Nina explores some of the complexities of human–gastropod relations through the story of a childhood memory. Nina as "Toddler-Me" is situated in a forest with her mother, picking chanterelles, and suddenly she finds herself surrounded by a group of snails. She describes a feeling of panic and fear: "No-one to save me from the snails, attacking me from everywhere – sneaking slowly in on me" (Ibid.). At the same time, Nina alternates in her writing between, on the one, hand the perspective of herself as a child – "Toddler-Me" – and, on the other hand, the imagined perspective of the snail. To me, this set in motion a multi-layered story of more-than-human considerations where the reader is not only presented with a story of human abjection but where the author also seeks to challenge this abjection by inviting the reader to imagine the same situation from the snail's perspective and through pleasure: "Snail pleasure – green, rainy, warm, wet snail pleasure. Intensely dripping trees; grass, leaves, mosses, everything so green, intensely green. I cannot escape. The circle of snails unbreakable. Spellbound, surrounded, totally stiff, I just stand there – and cry, cry, cry out loud" (Ibid.). To me, this is a powerful example of how storytelling has the capacity to explore the spaces and boundaries of fear of the alien and challenge the abject we might feel. This has the potential to open up other imaginaries and questions, which, in turn, can transform the ways that we feel for, think about, and sense with those creatures who are not the same as ourselves. This resonates deeply with me in my explorations of human–slug relations and is at the heart of the collaborative work and conversations involved in the making of our book.

Notes

1 "Vulgar slug" is the recommended name. Alternative names are "Spanish slug", "Iberian slug", "Lusitanian slug", "False Lusitanian slug", and "Plague slug" (Rowson et al. 2014, 36).
2 In 2021, the nickname *Mördarsnigeln* became Sweden's official name for this slug species, decided by SLU Swedish Species Information Centre (von Proschwitz et al. 2023).
3 Motion 2007/08:MJ321, Utbredningen av mördarsnigeln, Sveriges Riksdag, 2007.
4 Slugs and snails produce different mixtures of slime depending on purpose. If, for instance, the shell of a snail gets broken, the snail can release "a flood of lifesaving, medicinal mucus packed with antioxidants and regenerative properties" (Bailey 2010).
5 Email conversation October 28, 2020, with Ted von Proschwitz, senior curator, associate professor, Göteborg Natural History Museum, Sweden.
6 *Turning Over the Grounds of sgulS*, Katja Aglert, performance and photography with slugs, Sweden, 2017–2022.
7 Recorded interview in July, 2022 by Nina Lykke with Katja Aglert in Fur, Denmark.
8 Ibid.

Intertext II

Alien Arrivals

Diatoms

Nina Lykke

This is a collage of texts, written by Nina, Marietta[1], Katja, and Line at a writing workshop, organized as part of the work of the Alien Encounters Writing Collective that crafted this book. The automatic writing exercize which generated this text collage was prompted by photos of the diatomite cliffs of the island of Fur in the big Danish fjord, Limfjorden, as well as by a colourful piece of diatomite "rock" from the island that was placed physically before the participants. Moreover, Nina read a stanza aloud from her poem *A Pact* (see Chapter 3, this volume, and her monograph, *Vibrant Death*, Lykke 2022). The poem describes the moment when Nina's beloved lesbian life partner's ashes were scattered in the waters outside of Fur, and the island's amazing diatomite cliffs suddenly stood out to Nina.

Dreaming and Dying with Diatoms[2]

I came here in a dream – to the waters, to the waters, swimming among the brown, slimy algae. Never before have there been so many algae in the waters. They are sliding around my body while I swim. I feel them all over my body. I cannot see the bottom. It is a bit scary, but still I feel at home with you, here. At home among these soft, slimy, brown algae leaves that so gently caress my body. I cut my foot pretty badly when I walk in again. The stones are really sharp here. But I do not see the wound until I am sitting at the beach again after the swim. It is hot – and very different from last year. More dry on the top of the cliff, and more brown, and wildly growing algae in the water. Are there more stones as well? The pine tree that had fallen last year but which still had green pine needles is now totally grey brown. But it is still here. Other parts of the cliff have been eroded more – and a cave which I could enter earlier has now completely disappeared. Everything changes here. Changes from year to year. I keep thinking about how this place is going to be my grave – my ashes are to be scattered here when I die. This is certain. Uffe and Eigil have the coordinates. A strange feeling. Thinking again about Virginia Woolf's suicide. But I am not attracted to it now, as I was in the months right after

DOI: 10.4324/9781003373766-4

your death. The "come as ashes, not as flesh", which you whispered to me through the wind, while caressing my swimming body, has worked. I am attracted to this place, so attracted, but in a different way now. My attraction changes. Our relationship is ongoing. Your ashes, mixed with diatomaceous sand, cover the seabed, and when stirred up by the waves, it becomes one with the living diatoms, which also abound here. Since time immemorial, diatoms have lived and died and lived and died in these waters. I fell asleep, lying in the grass on the uttermost part of the cliff. Strange dreams merged with waking dreams. You are here. I love you. Ashes to ashes. Algae to algae. I am coming, my love. Forever, forever, dancing with diatoms at the bottom of the sea.

/N

Touching Diatomite Rock-not-Rock

LAYER UPON Layer, stripe upon stripe, layer upon layer and stripe upon stripe. The water comes closer and closer. The algae move back and forth, bodies touch bodies, become bodies, dissolve bodies.

Layers upon layers, stripes upon stripes.

Orange and grey, orange and grey, orange and grey.

Mo-clay.

Stones sunk in rock; not rock really but bodies upon bodies, stripes upon stripes.

Stones sticking out of rock; not rock really but bodies upon bodies, layers upon layers, stripes upon stripes.

Layers upon layers sixty metres high; how algae become archives; no longer resembling algae but recording year by year, month by month, day by day, keeping the thread alive while becoming dead. Bla blab la bla.

The spectrum of colours, dancing in the picture, in the rock-not-rock and stone–not-stone; tiny pebbles coming out of the rock-not-rock.

White and brown, yellow and green, grey and orange; pebble upon pebble, stone upon stone.

Who do you touch when you touch the stone; who do you touch when you touch the sedimented layer upon layer, stone upon stone.

One big cemetery, the forest of microscopic algae immortalised in the form of layer upon layer, stone upon stone.

You walk and walk and walk; the cliff stays there proud and untouched.

One big cemetery, the forest of microscopic algae immortalised in the form of layer upon layer, stone upon stone.

The cliffs don't cry; don't call for attention, don't act.

They are and they let be; like rocks; the lithic; the sedimental; the sign of time; the trace; the path of a once-there algae life; or rather the ever in/motion non/living.

/M

Wondering with Farting Fossils

Words, words, words, no and yes, they can only do so much. The imagined experience of this magical algae "rock" that evokes so many wonders and amazements. I want to explore its texture through words and immediately want to taste its surface. Full of small salty particles, like sandpaper, dry and yet sticky and perhaps a bit greasy like only salt and the sea can embody. I drown in all the nuances of colour tones, texture, scale, time, geology, layers, stories, not sure where to begin and at the same time completely satisfied with only being together with this piece of rock. In all its complexity, I capitulate and dive all in at the same time. It is again and again a mystery how we, humans that have only been here for so long, can claim so much about our ways of doing and thinking about things. I do the plunge back in time, down into deep time. Going into the micro world of algae. I find myself standing inside one of the pores of the rock in front of me and realize that the colour tones here from within are even more intense, golden, metallic, turquoise, jade green, okra, fire orange, orange orange, light as swan white-grey, algae green and a myriad of colours in between. It's not silent inside this algae rock, why did I assume that? It pops, the sound of oxygen bubbles popping, are the algae farting? Perhaps they have a sense of childish humour and laugh about farting in public? The smell is very mild in here, mineral salty, like ice can smell or perform a kind of non-smelling in its icy state. Only to become a more flowery, watery, gellyishi, fishy, wetty, smelly state in its fluid forms. What else? There is another sensation here inside, something beyond what I can put into words, something alien to me – so far. With this yet inexperienced sensation the algae take my hand, seem to show me the way to a place that I could never have imagined. Like playing the *Super Mario Bros* game where I drive on that psychedelic path. Bad comparison; this is like something that these words can never grasp. Like as if the brain, which apparently can not feel pain (or any other physical sensation) would suddenly experience something . . .

/K

Digesting with Giants and Ghosts

There's a doorway, and there's a staircase, both made for giants. There's saliva, there are teeth, and there are tongues. Fossilized giants. Teeth bursting from the ground. I think of us walking amongst such teeth. When that mouth shuts, what will happen to us? I can only see the lower teeth, the teeth of the lower jaw. Where, above us, in the night sky amongst sharp stars, is the upper jaw? The one with the sharp canines? The one that will come crushing down one night, in fire and dust and a rain of meteors? People will look up and realize that they are actually looking down, down into the guts of creatures older than they can even imagine. Millions, billions of years old. I don't understand it. I don't feel it. It is not in my guts, it is numbers on a page. It is thunder and lightning, meteors raining down from above and up from below, the sounds of millennia. Ghost sounds.

They haunt. My limited imagination haunts. The rocks – they wrap themselves around creatures, around the earth, around anyone and everyone, they swallow us whole, they keep us inside their guts. They are haunted ground. What ghost stories can we tell about cliffs? About rocks? About that which has been caught inside, that which is still among us, but abstract, vague, an imprint, a stripe, a colour, a taste of salt? I pick up a rocky staircase. I put it in my windowsill, and in the night, I find it in my doorway. Doorways. Staircases. "Where do I come from?" the stone says. We built these for giants. We built them for ourselves. "Where do I come from?" the rock insists. Dinosaurs walk the earth, and lightning the size of ocean floors floods the night sky. Now it all clusters around your kitchen, your windowsill. The giants hunch, they sit shoulder by shoulder, giant ghosts. Can you feel their breath on your cheek as you spread butter on your toast? Can you feel the soft touch of a fin, the fin of a ghost fish, billions and millions of years old, as it sails past your ankles? They are all here, the ghosts, they are massive, so massive, giant creatures of the universe, of time, of the Earth, of planets, of stars, all crammed in here, in your kitchen. I try to imagine all this as the rocks speak, and I know I fall short. I reach out, and I think of distances, and I think of time, and something breaks, and it hurts, and I've twisted my ankle, and the ghost fish whips past as if to say: we tripped you up. And sure, they did. I don't know how to live with the pressure of such vast timespans. Sometimes, I walk along the beach, it's a different beach this time, there are no cliffs, only sand and little stones, they hurt my feet. In the waters, there are fish and little shrimps, they eat the dead skin off of my feet. They pick it from the living flesh, carefully, carefully, sometimes getting it wrong so it smarts, it hurts. I think that to them, I might as well be a corpse. A massive ghost. A giant, bending the floors of their sea. To them, I may as well be dead. And I feed them – feet them, hah! Pun – and I wonder about the fish I've eaten during my life and the shrimps I had last night and how they must now be layered like rock formations, like stripes of dead white mass across my feet, and how that is what these tiny shrimps pick apart. The skeletal white remnants of their own kin. We give each other something, all of us, I suppose; the dead and the living, feeding each other. So many ghosts, they wander the earth. They walk with me on the beach. I no longer know what to say except I'm a giant, I'm massive, I crash and thunder into the realms of others, and I offer my flesh to them, and I know that that's a small gift from someone so big and that I'm a cheapskate.

/L

Notes

1 Marietta Radomska was part of the Alien Encounters Writing Collective that, together with the three co-authors of this volume, created the "Alien Arrivals: Diatoms" texts in an automatic writing workshop. We thank Marietta Radomska for her permission to publish her text "Touching Diatomite Rock-not-Rock" in this volume.

2 A considerably longer and somewhat different version of the text "Dreaming and Dying with Diatoms" has earlier been published as part of the prologue of the monograph Nina Lykke: *Vibrant Death*. London: Bloomsbury 2022, 3-4. It is reprinted here in accordance with the contractual agreement with the publisher.

3 Becoming a Compassionate Diatom Companion

Nina Lykke

Invitation to Diatoms

Will you dream and dance with me forever?
Will you touch me, when I die?
Will you eat me and digest me?
Can I live inside your guts?
And enjoy the sounds you make?
Wonder if they really mean
that you are farting . . .
Pop, pop, pop!
Pop-up, up, up!
Oh, my algae,
my companion,
let me co-become with you . . .

In the sci-fi-world shaped by Donna Haraway in the *Camille Stories*, the piece of narrative fiction which makes up part of her book *Staying With the Trouble* (Haraway 2016), it has become common to establish intimate relations of ethical accountability and kinship across species borders. The protagonist, Camille, has particular relations to the migratory Monarch butterfly. This implies that she pays special attention to the well-being of Monarch butterflies – and their possibilities for a vibrant, joyful, and sympoietic[1] entanglement with different habitats, corridors for migrating between them, and the world more broadly. The *Camille Stories* articulate Haraway's political vision of a future world where humans have become more-than-humans, living in, and feeling response-able for cross-species relations. I have established a relation of companionship with the micro-algae, diatoms, and feel aligned with Haraway's vision. This chapter tells the story of the coming into being of this companionship and the queer love relationship that unfolded from my attempts to co-become with diatoms as part of my eco-spiritual mourning practices.

My story is about mourning the cancer death of my lesbian life partner and about moving beyond what I call molar mourning. Molar mourning is focused

DOI: 10.4324/9781003373766-5

on the subject that was instead of embracing what I have defined as molecular mourning with inspiration from the immanence philosophy of Deleuze and Guattari (1988). According to Deleuze and Guattari, the molar frames the body as an organic whole and a fixed entity, while the molecular refers to the body as dissolved in its molecular processes of becoming. Against this background, I have defined molecular mourning as an effort to co-become with and attune to death's material metamorphoses and to the molecularization, dissolution into molecules, which death entails (Lykke 2022; Forthcoming c). The story deals with my queerfeminine efforts to materialize avid desires to co-become with the spiritmattering (Anzaldúa 2015; Schaeffer 2018) transformations of my queermasculine beloved's dead body when it was cremated to ashes and scattered over the sea in a place where living as well as dead (fossilized) diatoms abound, the waters outside of the island of Fur in the Danish fjord Limforden.

The story writing is inspired by methodologies of estrangement and defamiliarization, characteristic of speculative fabulation/science fiction (Bryld and Lykke 2000), more-than-human participatory research (Bastian et al. 2017), and decolonial research (Tlostanova 2023). In alignment with the overall theoretical framework of this book, I call upon estrangement and defamiliarization to sustain my story's articulation of the ways in which I have consciously tried to transgress nostalgic, molar mourning and instead attune to a spiritmattering, more-than-human, molecular shape-shifting alienness beyond anthropocentric and human exceptionalizing approaches to death and the corpse. As theorized in more detail in my poetic-philosophic monograph *Vibrant Death* (2022), I consider death as an ultimately alien condition, which we can never get to know beforehand. Moreover, I define this condition philosophically as vitally material in a bio- and geo-egalitarian sense (Bennett 2010; Braidotti 2006). This means that I want to avoid the exceptionalization of dead human bodies as different from any other dead matter and reject any dualist split of mind and body. In short, the alienness of the dead is to be understood as unexceptionally and vitally materially embodied. When someone dies to whom you have an intimate corpo-affective relationship, you are, as mourner, radically confronted with this strange alienness. As mourner, you can choose to stay in denial of the way in which the process of becoming-corpse is a process of becoming-alien. Or you can try to embrace and learn from it. I tried the latter route while digging into issues of molecularization together with the diatoms that I encountered.

The story on which the chapter is built moves through a sequence of vignettes which resonate with main stages of my process of becoming a compassionate diatom companion. The vignettes articulate the following stages: (1) Accepting my beloved's becoming-strange/estranged through her process of dying and moving beyond an existence as human subject.

(2) Choosing a place for the ashes scattering, which neither I nor my beloved had previously visited or known details about – a circumstance which opened an alien space for my mourning to unfold in a molecular mode without getting fixed in desires for a well-known molar past. (3) Unexpectedly, encountering diatoms, abounding in Limfjorden in fossilized as well as living shape and eventually engaging in a deeper and deeper spiritmattering and queer love relation and companionship with them. (4) Engaging other humans in diatom encounters and inviting both diatoms and other humans to become writing companions, as manifested among others in the "Alien Arrivals: Diatoms", Intertext II, this volume. (5) Comitting to diatom advocacy in the present times of mass extinctions and Anthropocene necropolitics (Lykke 2019b).[2]

Overall, the process of moving through the five vignettes takes me from reflections on compassionate and symphysizing (bodily empathizing) (Lykke 2022)[3] queer love for and companionship with my beloved to queer love for and compassionate and symphysizing, spiritmattering companionship with diatoms (dead and alive).

Vignette 1

Dying as Becoming-Alien

Excerpt from "Your Countenance"[4]

(Lykke 2022, 85–86)

Your moment of death had seemed calm. You had died with eyes half-closed, and your mouth a little bit open, forming a half-smile in the very moment of your last breath. Your dead body stayed in our house for thirtytwo hours until the undertaker brought us the ecological willow casket, and drove you away in it. As those hours went by, your countenance changed, congealing more and more. But still you kept looking at us with that unfathomable, Mona Lisa smile. My gut feeling told me not to interfere with your countenance. Intuitively, I felt that it would be utterly wrong and disrespectful to interfere with your face and follow the convention, which will have it that the eyes and mouth of the deceased should be closed. Why should we follow these conventions, invented to make the corpse look less corpse-like? Rebellious as you always were, you would definitely not have liked to have others meddling with your facial expression. Instead, your congealing half-smile – signifying the ultimate threshold between the "I" you were, and the corpse you were becoming – could perhaps tell me, the ignorant still living one, something about the crossing of this threshold.

But what happened to your countenance during those thirtytwo hours, when your dead body was still with us? What lessons in co-becoming did I learn? Can the series of photos which we took of you during these hours help me in this learning process? We took the photos in order to keep you with us, and I have regularly returned to them during the years that have now elapsed since you died. They are certainly important for my mourning through memorializing, as are all the photos of you that I have. However, these particular photos are important for something else as well – something that I still do not quite know-feel. These ultimately final photos of you in human shape show the changes over time of your countenance from the congealed half-smile of your moment of death towards something less and less "human"-looking and more and more unfathomable. This change is recorded with unanticipated clarity in the photos, and this is ultimately puzzling, forcing me to think-feel you in new ways. In my memory, you are still the one you were. But in the world of posthumous materiality, visually performed by these photos, you are coming to embody something else. I am struggling to find poetic, and philosophical words and ways to bring me closer to your posthumous materiality – to your vibrant death.

When I write this chapter, it is nine years after the ultimately devastating weeks of January 2014, where my forever beloved queermasculine lesbian life partner entered into the final process of dying and ultimate becoming-alien. It is eight and a half years after my first encounter with diatoms and the diatomite cliffs of the island of Fur in Limfjorden where we scattered my beloved's ashes in the summer of 2014. Early in December 2013, my partner was diagnosed with the disgustingly clinical word "terminal" and, on request, given the prognosis that she would die "between 2 weeks and 2 months" after, due to her final-stage small cell lung cancer that had metastasized irreversibly to her brain.

The above notes were written a couple of years later. At that time, I still experienced the mourning of my beloved as a very open wound. But I had also in-depth contemplated the spiritmattering event of the ashes scattering in the waters outside of the breathtaking Fur cliffs. During walks at the island, I had also learnt that the cliffs and the seabed there are made of diatoms, fossilized 55 million years ago on the threshold between the Paleocene and Eocene epochs of Earth's history. I had started to explore the wonders and enchantments of this place, where my ashes, too, in due time are going to be mixed into the assemblages of waters, diatomite seabed, sand, cliffs, living algae, seagrass, and oysters – assemblages with which my beloved's ashes are already entangled. When I wrote these notes, the event of the ashes scattering and the encounters with the cliffs, the fossilized diatoms that built them and the seabed, as well as with the living diatoms which abound in the waters of the fjord, had all started to work on me in a spiritmattering sense. Together with the diatoms – and oysters, which also have their habitat in the fjord and which were the alien presence that first attracted me to the place – I had begun to unfold my poetic-philosophic contemplations of death as a radical becoming-other, a becoming-inhuman, which is also a becoming-alien. I had started to wonder about the thrill and excitement of the alien encounters that this place gave me and the awe I felt when I wandered and swam there.

Moreover, I had reflected upon the ways in which my encounters with death's metamorphoses, which so visibly had changed my beloved's countenance after her last exhalation, were my first steps into a long process of spiritmattering co-becoming with this new habitat of my dead beloved's ashes (Lykke 2019a). A habitat which was completely alien to me but evidently home of so many other amazing (dead and living) creatures. I had delved into immanence philosophy (Braidotti 2006), material vitalism (Bennett 2010), and indigenous philosophy (Anzaldúa 2015). Through these philosophical forays, I had come to understand how all these underwater creatures perform their part of the cosmic dance of Zoe, the dynamic inhuman forces of vital matter that cross-cut the boundaries which conventional dualist thinking have used to separate the realms of life and death.[5]

When, in retrospect, I now ask myself how the life-changing event of my beloved's death and my intense mourning led me to the alien encounter with the diatoms, I see my intuitive resistance to interfere with her countenance as one of the crucial moments. My desire to let the utterly alien but so vibrant and not in any way uncanny or abject material presence of my beloved's dead body take the lead and teach me how to reconnect in new ways was already, back then, stronger than my desire to only mourn her in a molar mode as the embodied human subject she was. My feminist atheist, philosophical, and scientific beliefs had told me that my beloved's subject had become imperceptible and would not return in the human shape it had had. This shape might reappear in dreams and generate all kinds of spectral encounters, but only in ephemeral moments. The molar human was gone, and I was left with a devastating void and an aching, very fleshy feeling of pain. Still, my queerfeminine desires to abandon myself to the excitingly alien world into which I intuitively felt that my beloved's vibrant corpse could lead me were also awakened. So next to my devastated immersing myself in molar mourning of the subject that was, my desires to co-become with my beloved's becoming-molecular grew stronger in tandem with her metamorphozing from living human subject to dead corpse, ashes, and ashes-sand, mixed with the diatomaceous seabed of Limfjorden outside of the Fur cliffs.

The experience of my beloved's becoming-alien, but vibrant in a new way when she exhaled for the last time, is what, retrospectively, I consider to be one of the key moments in the chain of events which launched me into a queer love relationship and companionship with diatoms. At the time of my beloved's death, I knew nothing about diatoms, not even the name of this group of micro-algae was known to me. The following vignettes tell how my desire to follow my beloved to the alien worlds she was entering led me to these amazing and strange critters that built the Fur cliffs and seabed and fill the waters of Limfjorden today as well.

Vignette 2

From Oysters to Diatoms

Excerpt from "A Pact"[6]

(Lykke 2022, 134)

We let go of the line – our last tie to who you were before . . .
With a gurgling, slobbering slurping, the obscenity of which I know you would have loved,
the water swallows your blue ecological urn
to be dissolved at the seabed.
Swaddled in a sea-blue fishing net on a bed of oyster shells and beach stones,
you sink to the bottom of Limfjorden
outside of the cliffs of Fur,
close to the habitats of oysters.
The birth of Venus from the womb of the cliffs
in a reverse shot.
Roses gently rocking on the waves.
Somebody spots the head of a seal, enjoying the warm sun.
Naja reads from her story about a devil-may-care Karen Blixen.
We sing "You are so beautiful and gorgeous".

"I am coming, my love!"

When I wrote the poem "A Pact", which includes the above stanza about the sunny day in the summer of July 2014, where I, together with my rainbow family and close friends, sailed out on Limfjorden to scatter my beloved's ashes in the waters outside of the diatomaceous Fur cliffs, I still did not know anything about the diatoms. As mentioned, the reason we had chosen to scatter the ashes in these waters was the presence of oysters there – oysters which can become old and big and have a very special taste. The place is known for its particular kind of oysters, which have had their habitats there for thousands of years. Archeological excavations of prehistoric kitchen middens have shown that these oysters were part of the regular diet of the people who lived alongside of the fjord in prehistoric times. In the last weeks of my partner's life, it was difficult for her to eat, but oysters are light and nutritious, so we started to buy oysters from Limfjorden, which always had been a favourite dish of hers. She even became friends with an oyster fisher, who sent her the oysters. Trying to focus on oysters rather than on her rapidly approaching death, we also came to include oysters centrally in the story about reconnection which she and I developed together in these weeks, where both of us knew that death would tear us apart very soon after our 37 years of intimate bodily companionship. The story of reconnection grew strong between us. It took on miraculous qualities in ways which appeared as surprising even to ourselves, given our grounding in feminist atheism and secularism. Eventually, it developed into a pact, based on a mutual promise to do everything in our powers to meet again as grains of ashes, perhaps transformed to pearls by one of the many oysters of Limfjorden.

So oysters were, indeed, a key reason for the choice of Limfjorden as the place for the ashes-scattering. However, when contemplated retrospectively, it seems as if diatoms played an active role as well, albeit at the time unacknowledged by me. Firstly, there is a kind of metonymical link between oysters and diatoms. Morphologically, oysters appear as a kind of giant diatoms insofar as they repeat the structure with a shell covering a soft inside. Diatoms are unique among micro-algae, insofar as their protective encasement is a silica shell, called frustrule, which appears as multi-coloured as an effect of iridescence, when light is diffracted through minute markings of the diatom shell's nanostructures (Tiffany and Nagy 2019, 33–34). The beauty of these diatom shells has attracted the attention of phycology (the scientific study of algae) for several hundred years (Haeckel [1904] 2000) and resulted in diatoms being called "jewels of the sea" (Wikipedia 2023a). It is the shells of dead diatoms that, under certain circumstances, can give rise to fossil sediments such as the 60-meter-thick ones that have shaped the seabed and multi-coloured cliffs of the Fur Formation. So the shells make the diatoms unique and create a link between them and the oysters that first called me to the fjord.

Secondly, the moment of lowering the dissolvable ecological urn with the ashes into the water and letting go of the line with which we held it created a strong both visual and auditive relation to the two biggest diatomaceous cliffs of Fur. The captain who took us on his boat to the place where we scattered the ashes, had been sailing in these waters for years and knew exactly how to position the boat favourably. He dropped anchor about 400 to 500 meters from the cliffs so that we could look directly at the two biggest of these when we lowered the urn into the water. It was a warm and quiet day, and the sun shone from a cloudless sky. The cliffs stood out very clearly against the blue heaven – and the view was magical. From the seaside, the cliffs look like the upper part of the thighs and the mound of Venus of a woman lying with a sexually open vulva. At least this is what I saw when I let go of the line to the urn – packed into a fishing net with beach stones and oyster shells to give it more weight in order to make sure that it would sink to the bottom before the ecological material it was made of would dissolve and unleash the ashes to swim freely. Moreover, to make it sensuously even clearer that this was a sexual return to the womb from where we all arrive to life as newborns, the slurping sound of the waters swallowing the urn was as if it came from a gigantic orgasming vulva full of wet juices. Can you imagine a better hydrofeminist and lesbian burial?

In the midst of my utterly devastated condition, I felt so happy about the way in which the moment of letting go of the line materialized – this moment that was so symbolically laden as well as physically real, the moment of my beloved's transition into the ultimately alien world of the dead. Until then, I had somehow been responsible for the decisions about what should happen to her dead body in order to fulfill our mutual pact of trying, if possible, to find ways to reconnect. I had taken so much care of her dead body and, later, the urn, which I received from the undertaker after the cremation. Now these tasks were completed, and her ashes were on their own, totally beyond my control. But the magical view of the cliff/mound of Venus and the accompanying sexual sound of the waters embracing the urn made me feel that the ashes were warmly welcomed to their new – to me, the still-living mourner, so very alien – habitat. As mentioned, I did not know much about this habitat and its inhabitants at the time beyond the fact that it was the home of many oysters. But retrospectively, the moment of unleashing the ashes into the water and experiencing how it was received by the assemblage of cliffs and water stands out to me as my first powerful encounter with the alien world of diatoms, even though I still did not know anything about these critters.

Vignette 3

Listening to the Ancestral Wisdom of Diatoms

Since we scattered my beloved's ashes in the waters outside of the Fur cliffs, I have visited this place every summer, feeling my beloved holding me while swimming in the waters and walking both beneath and on top of the cliffs. This is how I became consciously aware of the diatoms. At my first walk at the beach beneath the cliffs, my eyes were caught by the colours and the strangely mosaic look of the cliffs. It was as if the cliffs were composed of small, differently coloured pieces of a gigantic jigsaw puzzle, every one of them separated from the others by distinct edges. They looked very different from both rocky cliffs and cliffs made by ordinary clay.

The jigsaw puzzle image was reinforced when I looked at the beach in front of the cliffs. The closer I came to the cliffs, the more the beach abounded with multi-coloured "stones" which had the same very distinct edges as the ones that composed the cliffs. When I took these beach "stones" in my hand, I discovered that they were very light, much lighter than rock, but also that they broke pretty easily into pieces that could be fitted exactly together precisely like those of a jigsaw puzzle. Never ever had I seen "stones" like that before. Excited to find such enigmatic stones in the place, which already appeared as enchanted to me due to the ways in which it was part of the assemblages which now also were the habitat of my beloved's ashes, I began to wonder about the messages and stories these jigsaw puzzle "stones" carried. I started avidly to pick them up and fill my backpack with them, hoping that they would tell me something. In particular, I was enchanted by a type of white "stones" with yellow stripes. It was as if a mystery emanated from these particular "stones". The yellow stripes somehow suggested that they framed a

Figure 3.1 Jigsaw Puzzle . . . Diatomite cliffs, Fur, Limfjorden, Denmark.
Source: © Nina Lykke 2021.

picture, but within the frame, the whitish-greyish "stone" mass just repeated itself. Was this whitish-greyish mass within the yellow frame the message? It was as if an icon with metonymic relations to something important but very alien and unfathomable presented itself to me without putting itself immediately on display.

Figure 3.2 Enigmas within Yellow Frames . . . Diatomite cliffs, Fur, Limfjorden, Denmark.

Source: © Nina Lykke 2023.

The enchanting enigmas of these "stones" and the jigsaw-puzzle-like appearance of the cliffs prompted me to delve into the geo- and biohistory of the Fur Formation. I visited the local natural history museums, where the geological history of the diatomite cliffs and seabed is elaborately described. I also began eagerly to read scientific literature on diatoms, diatomite, the Fur cliffs, and the deep time formation of Fur and the surrounding seabeds and seascapes. I read about the coming into being of cliffs and seabed, when dead and fossilized diatoms sedimented in thick layers at the bottom of the subtropical sea that covered the area at the threshold between the Paleocene and the Eocene epochs of the planet's history, around 55 million years ago (Sharma 1969; Pedersen 1981; Bonde 2008). I learnt that back then, there was a lot of volcanic activity in the area, and I found out that geologists have counted approximately 180 layers of volcanic ashes cutting through the 60-meter-thick layer of sedimented diatomite that makes up cliffs and seabed (Pedersen 1981). These studies also helped me to become skilled in distinguishing between different kinds of diatomite, and I learned that the white diatomite "stones" with the framings of yellow stripes have a particular, dramatic geo-biological history. They testify to the occurrence of large-scale anoxic events happening occasionally 55 million years ago due to massive volcanic eruptions which, now and then, produced gigantic ash clouds that shadowed the sun so that plants and photosynthesizing algae (including diatoms) were cut off from their sources of nutrition and died en masse. It dawned on me that the white pieces of diatomite with yellow stripes could be understood as relics that put me metonymically in touch with diatom mass death as part of these dramatic deep time events.

However, I also came to understand that these yellow-striped white "stones" told a story about resilience and ongoingness. The grey-black layers of ashes, so visible on the sides of the cliffs, shifted with layers of whitish or coloured diatomite. In this way, the layers told a story about continuous shifts between, on the one hand, periods of anoxic events and mass death following the volcanic eruptions and the spreading of ash clouds and, on the other hand, periods, where ongoing algae life/death cycles unfolded. The massive shifts that thus seemed to have taken place on a regular and ongoing basis opened my horizon towards a story about the big cycles of ongoingness and diatom resilience that cross-cut the history of the planet. Diatoms are assumed to have come into being in the Jurassic, and they are still around today, so they have performed myriads of life/death cycles since then. Furthermore, my contemplations of the diatomite cliff walls and beach-"stones" made me think about the ways in which the catastrophe of individual death that my molar mourning circled around, from the cliffs' perspective, is part of overall ongoing processes of molecular vibrant becomings, of ongoing shifts between becoming and decomposing which make up the dynamic forces of Zoe. The cliffs made the immanence philosophical point palpably clear that processes of decomposing/death and recomposing/life are not opposites but completely entangled in each other – a point which resonated with biophilosopher Marietta Radomska's reconceptualization of life/death as non/living (2020). Together with my scientific studies of diatoms and philosophical reflections on vibrant materiality and immanence, the contemplation of the cliffs also brought me to consider that not only was reconnection with my beloved, ashes to ashes at the bottom of Limfjorden, possible but also likely. When my ashes are scattered there, they will enter into the same world of Zoe-defined ongoingness (Braidotti 2006) of which those of my beloved are already part. I coined the concept of vibrant death (Lykke 2022) to define the generative kind of death, which is implied here, that is death as a vibrant merging with the dynamic forces of Zoe that are immanent to the material world, in preparation for a cyclical/spiralling shape-shifting reemergence. Along this road, I also came to understand the importance of a total reevaluation of the ancestral wisdom of diatoms (Lykke 2019a, 2022; Hazekamp and Lykke 2022).

Vignette 4

Engaging Human Companions in Spiritmattering Human–Diatom Relations

Excerpt from "Fur"[7]

(Lykke 2022, 101–103)

I feel like swimming.
The water folds smoothly around my body.
I am floating on my back
looking up into the sky.
You hold me,
while I swim with long, long back strokes.
Then my gaze is drawn
by the blue, red, yellow, black, white stones of the cliff,
a gigantic abstract painting,
created by enormous dynamic forces,
diatomfossil on diatomfossil,
fiftyfive million years of vibrating geological history
condensed into a sixty-metre high cliff,
erase every meaningful distinction
between life and death.

The Intertext "Alien Arrivals: Diatoms" preceding this chapter includes a cluster of poetic texts written as automatic writing pieces at a writing workshop that took place as part of the crafting of this book. The prompts I had prepared for the workshop were a piece of red, grey, and white diatomite from Fur and the above lines from my poem "Fur" (Lykke 2022, 101f.) that contemplates my first walks at the cliffs after the ashes-scattering. These were the walks where I encountered the diatoms and started to desire to become their companion. While preparing for the workshop, I wondered if the two prompts could make my human writing companions begin to share my attraction to and amazement about the diatoms. Were the vibrancies of the diatomite strong enough to work at a distance, so to speak – that is, could I call forth the magic only through the piece I had brought home with me from Fur and through the words of my poem? The automatic writing pieces from the workshop confirmed that the answer to that question was a yes: the spiritmattering vibrancy of the diatoms came to pervade the workshop space through the automatic writing pieces. I felt that it was possible to share wonder, enchantment, and amazement with my human writing companions and that their responses also opened exciting new horizons for me in terms of a further unfolding and deepening of my companionship and process of co-becoming with the diatoms.

Let me foreground some key themes which stand out when I contemplate how the written texts from the workshop envision alien encounters between diatoms and humans while firmly transgressing the gap which such encounters conventionally are supposed to signal. This is a gap between highly "developed", "complex", "exceptionally embrained and superior" multicellular humans and "primitive", "simple", "inferior" single-cell diatom-organisms. This gap has been constituted through the normative modes of telling the history of biological evolution as a development from simplicity to complexity (Schrader 2012), that is: using a narrative scheme which confirms human exceptionalism, making us (humans) appear as the peak of evolution. The collectively written "Alien Arrivals: Diatoms" texts share a commitment to radically undo this gap, and one of their undoing-strategies is to turn the vertical relationship of humans and diatoms around. This is manifested, for example, in Katja's text, when its textual "I" makes herself small enough to enter the piece of red, grey, and white diatomite, which I had placed in front of us while we wrote. A similar move is performed in Line's text, when its "I" sees herself as part of a diatomaceous giant of cosmic proportions.

A related mode of transgressing the gap is to make a dual move of critically exposing the destructive work of the bio- and geo-historical chronologies which underpin the distance between diatoms and humans and affirmatively undoing it through shifts of temporal or spatial perspectives (Lykke Forthcoming d). Such moves are performed both in Katja's and Line's texts in the "Alien Arrivals: Diatoms" Intertext. On the one hand, the time of Chronos (chronological time, as manifested, for example, in the shape of the history of biological evolution or the history of Earth's geological evolution) is, by both Katja and Line, foregrounded as that which makes the diatoms distant to "us" (humans), insofar as it blocks the possibilities for corpo-affective communication on a geo- and bioegalitarian basis. Katja's text, for example, speaks about "drown[ing]" in "time" and "geology" and feeling the need to "capitulate". In a somehow similar vein, the "I" of Line's text states that she does not understand creatures being "millions, billions of year old", because she cannot "feel it" – "it is not in my guts. It is numbers on a page". However, on the other hand, another temporality appears as a textual solution in both Katja's and Line's text – a temporality which is different from the abstractly

Figure 3.3 Giant's Teeth . . . Diatomite cliffs, Fur, Limfjorden, Denmark.

Source: © Katja Aglert and Nina Lykke 2023.

forward-running time of Chronos, which creates distance and hence feelings of stuckness, when the textual "I" tries to establish corpo-affective relations to the diatoms. In Katja's text, the "I" all of a sudden finds herself "standing inside one of the pores of the rock in front of me" after having done "the plunge back in time, down into deep time"; Katja's "I" stands there not in order to record a chronological sequence of eons and epochs but to enter into what I suggest to theorize as an Aionic moment. Here, I refer to the non-chronological time of the instant that Deleuze (2020, 167–172) defines as the time of Aion and opposes to the time of Chronos. In Katja's text, the Aionic moment is textually performed as a bodily entering the "micro world of algae" in order to experience its colours, sounds, tactile qualities, tastes and smells from within and to let "the algae take [her] hand" and "show [her] the way to a place that [she] could never have imagined". In Line's text, it is another spatiality which creates a textual possibility to undo the blockages set up by Chronos. Line's text thus transforms the gap between the time when the cliffs were built and present-day time into a cosmic space made up of giant bodies. Both ways of undoing the time of Chronos (through the Aionic moment or through the enigmatic spatiality of a cosmos perceived as bodies) open for sensuous contemplations and desiring, embodied co-becomings with the alien world of diatoms.

A further transgressive strategy is to undo any kind of exceptionalizing and hierarchizing human presence, conceptualized within the framework of a flat ontology which also undoes the opposition between life and death in favour of a cyclical ongoingness. This move manifests itself in my own text in the "Alien Arrivals: Diatoms", Intertext II, when it ends in an eternal dance of critters inhabiting the seabed: "Forever, forever dancing with diatoms at the bottom of the sea". The dissolution of any presence specifically marked as human performed against the background of a flat ontology, links also to the rhythmic repetitions "layer upon layer and stripe upon stripe" of Marietta's text in the "Alien Arrivals: Diatoms" Intertext. The repetitions performed here suggest that ongoing, cyclical shifts between life and death will go on and on, entangled in each other as "the ever in/motion non/living" and without atten-tion to the human presence of the textual "you" who walk and walk, while "the cliff stays there proud and untouched". An ongoingness beyond the life/death threshold, also framed within a flat ontology, appears in Line's "Alien Arrivals: Diatoms" Intertext, too, filled as it is not only with giants but also with ghosts and spectres of more-than-human critters such as "ghost fish". In their own hauntological and ephemeral but still phenomenal way, ghosts and spectres mediate between what is conventionally defined as an opposition between the living and the dead, while, in a Derridean sense (1994), they also completely undo this opposition.

Vignette 5

Becoming a Diatom Advocate

So my diatom-companions brought me to reevaluate their ancestral wisdom, and, together with my human writing companions, I delved into celebra-tions of their resilient commitment to cyclic ongoingness. Still, what if the cycles of ongoingness become definitively broken and vibrant dying is prevented from taking place? There is a pressing need to attend to this question when confronted with today's ecological crises. Therefore, I dedicate this last vignette to a contemplation of the waves of species and ecosystem extinctions caused by contemporary human, capitalist, and post/colonial, interventions in the planet's metabolism, which I elsewhere have discussed as Anthropocene necropolitics (Lykke 2019b). The necropolitical processes are today so globally over-arching that local extinctions as the ones that occasionally hit diatoms on the threshold between Paleocene and Eocene due to volcanic eruptions are adding massively up so that there are less and less spaces for refuge and regeneration of conditions that can secure ongoingness (Haraway 2016). So it becomes urgent to ask: How to prevent what critical extinction studies scholar and ecoactivist Deborah Bird Rose aptly called double-death (2012, 128) and aenocide (2012, 137) (that is: the definitive disruption of regeneration cycles) from becoming the global norm rather than an occasional occurrence?

To avoid ending in total gloom and doom, this train of thought brought me back to Haraway's reflections on companionship and to her suggestion (2016), which I quoted in the introduction to this chapter, about taking responsibility for relations to specific critters. This suggestion resonates with Rose's argument for advocacies that take a point of departure in embodied and concrete relations to named animals, plants, etc. (2017) rather than to "nature" as abstraction. The particular relation becomes metonymically related to the planetary assemblage of nature and culture – standing in for this total assemblage as *pars pro toto* (part for the whole), but, importantly, in an embodied and concretely relational sense. For me, the diatoms have become such embodied and concrete companions for whom I want to do advocacy. The history of my relation to them implies that I have extended my queerfeminine sensibilities towards my queermasculine beloved to the assemblages of which her ashes have become part. My advocacy for diatoms is based on the queer love relationship that I have developed to them.

At the same time, I note that diatoms are among the thousands and thousands of species for which advocacy is urgently needed in the contemporary world (Lykke 2019a, Forthcoming a). When seabeds in diatom-rich coastal waters located close to mass polluting agro-businesses, for example, die permanently, then diatoms die, too. The phenomenon of seabeds in coastal waters, threatened by permanent extinction, is occurring widely today – from Limfjorden to the Gulf of Mexico. I try both to teach myself and to wonder about how to make broader publics break out of the normative standard of indifference towards minute alien critters such as diatoms that appear as evolutionarily distant, utterly alien and unimportant to "us" (humans). I try to teach myself and others that diatoms are crucial for "our" lives insofar as they annually produce 25% to 50% of the planet's oxygen. But, in particular, I try to emphasize that we should begin to care about them in a non-utilitarian sense – as wise ancestors and more-than-human

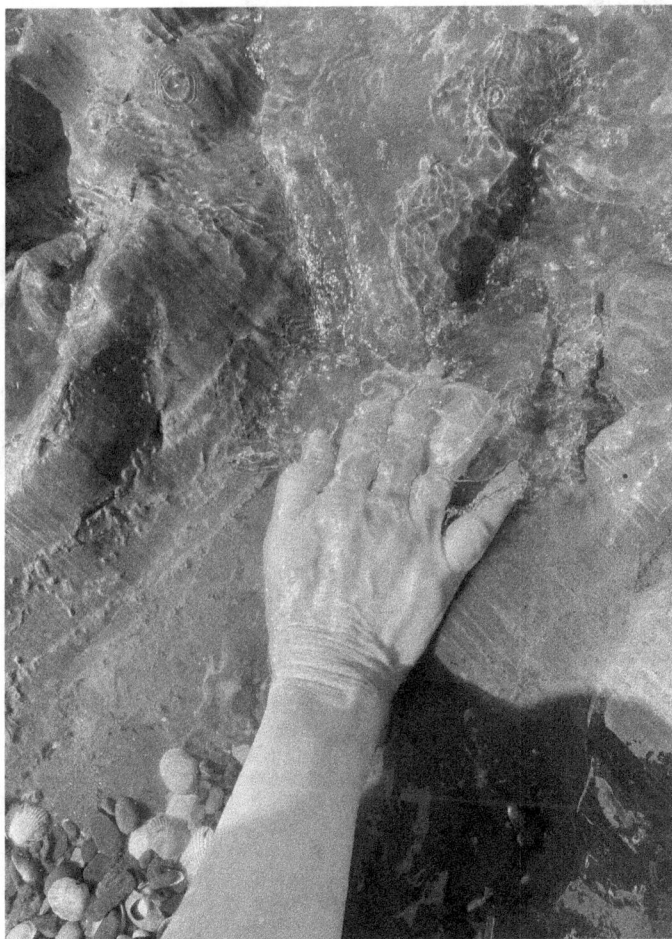

Figure 3.4 To Touch and Be Touched . . . Diatomite seabed, Fur, Limfjorden, Denmark.

Source: ©Katja Aglert and Nina Lykke 2023.

companions with whom we are horizontally conjoined in networks of sympoietic mutuality.

Notes

1 *Sympoiesis* is a key term in Haraway's reontologizing of planetary relations, based on kinship (2016, 58–99). While the concept of autopoiesis refers to self-organizing organisms, the notion of sympoiesis (deriving from Greek "making-with") emphasizes

the ways in which all organisms enfold each other rather than develop independently of their "environment". The notion of *sympoiesis* undoes the idea of an individual and its environment as separate entities.

2 The concept of *Anthropocene necropolitics* (Lykke 2019b) draws on the ways in which the notion of Anthropocene, "the age of man", has become a buzzword, indicating a shift of geological age taking place due to significant, human-induced alterations of processes of planetary metabolism. This shift is currently discussed by geologists, but the concept has also entered the sphere of political critique. The critical use of the Anthropocene concept by scholars in the humanities and social sciences points to the "accelerating extinctions across all biological taxa and also multispecies, including human, immiseration across the expanse of Terra" (Haraway 2016, 46). Lykke (2019b) combines this critical use of the Anthropocene concept with the notion of necropolitics, coined by postcolonial scholar Achille Mbembe (2003). Providing historical examples from the Holocaust and the plantations driven by slave labour, Mbembe theorizes the ways in which the establishment of sovereign power in modernity installs regimes of life and death that make certain bodies disposable, exposing them to potentially deadly conditions, while other bodies are made to live well and to be saved at all costs. Mbembe's focus is human bodies. The linking of his concept to the notion of Anthropocene foregrounds the ways in which the distinction disposable/non-disposable is relevant also when it comes to thinking about relations between human and other-than-human bodies (Lykke 2019b; Radomska, Mehrabi, and Lykke 2020).

3 The concept *symphysizing* is developed in Lykke (2018, 2022) with reference to what philosopher Ralph Acampora defines as *symphysis* (Acampora 2006, 76), that is: an embodied, Spinoza-inspired rethinking of the notion of sympathy, which stresses the component of corpo-affectivity. Coining the concept of *symphysis*, Acampora underscores that the relation is not only a question of feeling for and caring about the other; it is also implied that the subject, in a material, corpo-affective sense, is affected by and co-experiences the ways in which hir significant other/s are bodily affected. Translating symphysis into verb form, *symphysizing*, Lykke (2018, 2022) stresses that the bonding between companions builds upon ongoing, intercorporeal, and affective processes and not upon a static relationship, defined once and for all.

4 The text is an excerpt from a longer poetic text, earlier published in Nina Lykke. *Vibrant Death*. London: Bloomsbury 2022, 85–86. It is reprinted here in accordance with the contractual agreement with the publisher.

5 The concept of *Zoe* is used in line with feminist philosopher Rosi Braidotti's redefinition of this Aristotelian concept. Braidotti takes the understanding of *zoe* in a non-anthropocentric direction, focusing on *zoe*'s "generative powers" against the background of an immanence philosophical approach. Braidotti redefines the concept as part of a radically bio- and geo-egalitarian "eco-philosophy of multiple belongings" (Braidotti 2006, 39–41). Within this framework, *zoe* is to be understood as "the endless vitality of life as continuous becoming", which grounds the human subject as an "ecological entity", transversally and transcorporeally related to all other planetary existences, both human and non-human (Ibid.)

6 The text is an excerpt from a longer poetic text, earlier published in Nina Lykke. *Vibrant Death*. London: Bloomsbury 2022, 134. It is reprinted here in accordance with the contractual agreement with the publisher.

7 The text is an excerpt from a longer poetic text, earlier published in Nina Lykke. *Vibrant Death*. London: Bloomsbury 2022, 101–103. It is reprinted here in accordance with the contractual agreement with the publisher.

Intertext III

Alien Arrivals

Familiars

Line Henriksen

This is a collage of text excerpts written by Katja, Marietta,[1] Nina, and Line. It is edited by Line. The writing prompt was: (1) Have a look at the painting *Mad Meg* (1563) by Pieter Bruegel (see Figure 4.1, this volume). Is there a creature in there you might like to summon as your familiar spirit? (2) Write non-stop for 10 minutes – no editing, no polishing – from that creature's perspective.

Though the text has been edited, Line has, to a large extent, kept the polishing to a minimum, meaning that there may be some strange sentences and just a bit of oddness here and there, which seems truthful to the automatic writing used to produce the text.

"They Call it Extinction and Apocalypse – Hell. I Call it Breakfast"

(Quote by Nina)

I am not an I, but multiple organisms that can form
shape
into whatever they like.
I devour.
The smell and taste.
Red lips.
I devour
human flesh for breakfast every day. This is heaven, not Hell.
How does it taste?
A bit sweet when it is eaten raw.
I devour I devour I devour I
am not an I, but multiple
I am a fairly big fish
I am a castle
I am a rock
I am rock'n'roll
I play the electric guitar

DOI: 10.4324/9781003373766-6

I squeak
I scream
I am eating everyone alive

(Oh oh they interviewed the creature)

The Creature Says

"Welcome to Hell – the gate is a mouth, an open mouth, my mouth, I devour; the slimy mouth, watering mouth. I devour; I swallow – once you enter the gate there is no way out. I devour. Welcome to Hell, I devour. There are all those little bastard humans. I devour. The smell and taste. I devour. The actual frame of the gate to Hell, a gate in Hell. I devour. My eyes are always on a lookout; eyes of a mountain. I devour. I keep on looking around. A mountain staring around. I devour. A day after day after day another day and night, after night, another night. I devour a week after week another week, and one more week. I devour and month after month another month and yet one more month. I devour. And year after year, another year and one more year. I devour. Eternal cycle. Repetition with a difference, repetition that makes a difference, difference that makes a repetition; difference that makes repetitions. I devour. I, the mountain, a gate in Hell or a gate to Hell, your Hell, am surrounded by a wall. What kind of architect dares to try to capture me? But walls fall down. I devour. Come over here, oh yes, over here, into the gate, a gate in Hell; look at my orange red lips. I devour. Look at the beauty of my teeth. I devour. Become one with the slime. Smell its sweet stench. I might need to close one day but for the time being I devour".

/M

The Creature Says

"I like to sneak up on these humans who are so clumsy when in water. So I sneak up on them and scare the shit out of them. They know that I am capable of swallowing them up in one go. MMMMMMMMMMMM. One more human – but I do not like their clothes. They should go naked. This would make them more eatable. I am a big fish – a big white fish, I have big eyes and a big mouth. Do I have a big brain? This is what these human guys sometimes ask when I hear them converse in their stupid language on the brink of the river. The only thing that counts for them is what they call brains, and this shows how amazingly stupid they are. Why do they not ask about other things? Instead of talking amongst themselves, they could ask me what I feel when I swim – or how I experience the taste of their flesh. Do I want them to pay attention to other things than their stupid human perspectives? Frankly, I do not care. What I care about is their amazing taste, which really caresses my palate. I am a big white fish – living in the sea, in the rivers, everywhere – in the rivers of what they call Hell – the river Styx, the river of forgetfulness.

I am called a liminal creature by the humans – because I live in this river, which is located precisely on the threshold between their life and their death. But again, isn't this a totally stupid and self-centred argument. Because I am really thriving here – I am not on a threshold. The threshold is theirs, not mine".

/N

The Creature Says

"Magic takes skill! It takes words! It takes sustenance! What are all these books anyway? Let's see . . . tastes like dust. Tastes like cardboard. Tastes like discourse analysis. Have you ever considered what magic might do for you in your line of work? I swear, you're lucky I showed up. Maybe I summoned you, eh? You never know! Anyway, let's see what we can do. Let's see what we can write. Let's see how we can use magic as a tool. Let's open a book. Let's add an egg. Use some flour to cradle it all. Sit on it for a few minutes, like a mother hen. Magic work takes love. It takes dedication. It takes a warm bum. Now, open the book, take out a few pages, cook at 170°, and then you open the oven, and you can move right in, you can walk right through, slide on your belly like a worm, and then you are where you want to be! You have moved into new terrain, and remember to bring the cooked book! It's important! Hold the cooked book pages close to heart and nibble at them, as long as you nibble at them nothing can harm you, nothing can take your soul and boil it and season it and roast it in butter and mushroom until crunchy and nice and hmmmmmmmmmmmmm. . . . Anyway, keep nibbling at the book, and before you're out of book, find the nearest oven, turn it to 170° and move through it, and you'll be back with me, safe and sound. That's the only way to cook and frankly it's the only way to read too. Now, what's for breakfast? What's for lunch? I'm starving and I've not been able to get a word in edgewise this whole time, do you ever shut up . . ."

/L.

The Creature Says

"This was a very hard task.
It is a laugh.
It is a nightmare.
It is poison.
It is toxic, eats everyone alive, smells horrible, is the hunger of all hungers, the heat of all heats.
This is just a horrible experience.
The scream, the hole, the tunnel, the gap, the entrance to a dream, to a nightmare, the club, the rave, the LSD, the sauna, I feel the madness, the dance, the cliché, the absinth, bla bla, plack, pack, neck, deck. I am

warm as Hell inside and the sweat of my nostrils drip like honey down on everyone that dares to enter my interiors.

The individuals moving around in my interiors tickle my feet but from the inside. Bla bla bla bla bla bla bla bla bla aha

I have really no idea.

And I have never had so much trouble writing".

/K.

Note

1 Marietta Radomska was part of the Alien Encounters Writing Collective that, together with the three co-authors of this volume, created the "Alien Arrivals: Familiars" texts in an automatic writing workshop. We thank Marietta Radomska for her permission to publish her text in this volume under the title "The Creature Says", signed "M".

4 Writings from the Pit

On Creative Blocks and the Internal Editor as Familiar Spirit

Line Henriksen

Invitation to the Familiar
I'm using this mouse –
this one, you can't see it but imagine a small grey knitted mouse, little round body,
small tail, it fits in the palm of my hand. During Christmas it lives in a little red hat,
a nissehue, and the rest of the year it lives here, on my desk, and when the voice
picks up, when I start editing and editing until there is nothing more to edit because
all is gone, when that happens, I take the little grey mouse in my hand and
I place it in a little blue sock and
I put it on my desk
facing away from me and
I say the words, the incantation, I say:
"you don't need to work now, you know,
you don't need to protect me
in the sock".

Nigel

Whenever I write, there is that little voice at the back of my head going: "Are you sure that is a good way to start a chapter? Do we really like that word? Couldn't you be spending your time better doing something else?" The voice is well known and theorized in work on creative as well as academic writing (see, for example, Koobak 2014; Burroway 2014; Anzaldúa 2015) and is typically referred to as the internal editor or critique. In an interview on the joys and difficulties of writing, writer Julia Cameron explains how she calls her own internal editor "Nigel" (France and Romolini 2023, 33:31–33:33), which is one way to pin down and give shape to it, or as she puts it: "miniaturize your censor" (Ibid., 17:10–17:13). Interestingly, Cameron does not suggest getting rid of the censor, only miniaturizing it, as if ridding oneself of this voice is not necessarily possible – maybe not even desirable?

This chapter is my attempt at and very small step towards exploring and perhaps even slightly improving my relationship with my own overly critical

DOI: 10.4324/9781003373766-7

internal editor voice, my own Nigel, since ridding myself of it seems unlikely at this point; we go way back. It is also an attempt at sharing my own experiences of living with a run-amok internal editor, in case my experiences are of use to others living and creating with (and in spite of) similar voices. Nigel has become an inherent part of any writing project I take on, and I do need to take on writing projects, it is part of my job, but when Nigel is at its best – perched on my shoulder, asking me to "delete, delete, delete, for the love of God, delete, don't let anyone see that, it's positively obscene!" – it can mean endlessly deferred deadlines, projects piling up, never to be finished because I become overwhelmed, and ultimately a complete halt in my academic and creative work. Our personal record, mine and Nigel's, is taking four years to write a 1,000-word essay. Need I say that as I am writing this, Nigel and I have been editing and revising this chapter to Hell and back and that today is the deadline for it being fully finished, and we are nowhere near getting there? (Nigel would like you to know that despite what it might seem, as you are right now reading the chapter, we did, in fact, never get there.)

The tools of psychology have been of help when it comes to improving my relationship with Nigel. "Could you externalize the voice?" a counsellor once asked and pointed to a collection of plastic animals she had on her shelves. "Give it a form?" I thanked her for the offer of a miniature animal but instead chose a small, knitted mouse I already had on my desk at home. I imagined it to be the editor, and whenever its voice became too loud, I put it in a sock and turned it away from my laptop, telling it to shush and that all was well. The thing about Nigels, I have come to realize, is that they do not do their editorial work out of malice. In their own unhelpful way, they try to help by making sure that whatever you do, you do not open yourself up to criticism, which – in their beady eyes – does not just mean a mere inconvenient bit of editing but the complete loss of any kind of worth. Danish author and stand-up comedian Sofie Hagen explains it well in a YouTube conversation, where they talk about their own internal editor voice telling them they should feel bad about being fat: "What our brain is always doing, even though it sometimes does it awfully, is it will always try and keep you safe", they say, continuing:

> So your brain thinks that if it just tells you "you look fat, this is bad", then you are warned, and then you are ready for, like, fat-shaming or whatever . . . so sometimes you have to become the parent of the voice. Be like, "Hey, I know that you are doing this because you are wanting to protect me, but we know better now. And actually, everything is absolutely fine. I don't even need your help anymore . . ." It's not trying to hurt you.
>
> (Hagen 2023, 27:00–27:50)

In Cameron's and Hagen's stories, the internal critique seems to have a mind of its own; it is part of but in excess of its person, and its attempts at help and protection stem from previous wounds, from feelings of vulnerability, from fears and anxieties about how one's work, one's body, one's entire sense of self will be received by the world and therefore how or if the self gets to be loved and accepted. There is something about this agency and companionship that, to me, can be partly grasped by the language of psychology, for example, through the plastic or knitted animal companions. But there is also something about my relationship with Nigel that is in excess of this language, something weirdly creature-like, even alien, that I am still trying to figure out. In an attempt to address this excess, I turn to folklore: the unhelpful helping and unwavering companionship as well as the slight sense of the more-than-human (I mentioned Nigel being perched on my shoulder since this is how Cameron experiences it: "Perched on your shoulder, saying: this isn't good enough" [France and Romolini 2023, 17:20–17:23], making it bird-like and definitely not completely human) reminds me of the witch's familiar; the demonic spirit that aids the spellcaster in their magic, at a price.

Beëlphazoar

To speak of the familiar, not least of the editor-as-familiar, I would like to begin with a story I came across more than a decade ago and which stuck with me: *The Disrespectful Summons* (1980), an illustrated poem by American author Edward Gorey. It tells the story of Miss Squill, who is struck down by the Devil and receives his mark on her chest as well as a familiar in the shape of a small, winged creature called Beëlphazoar. Through the poem and its illustrations, we follow the domestic lives of Miss Squill and Beëlphazoar: they cook;

"It brought a recipe for fudge
Of pounded pencil-stubs and sludge"

they read in bed, Beëlphazoar comfortably tucked away by Miss Squill's feet;

"Also a book called Ninety-two
Entirely Evil Things To Do"

they redecorate their home;

"She got from somewhere stones with eyes
And plants that gave out screams and sighs"

and they murder their neighbours;

"She did her neighbours' forms in wax
And stuck them full of pins and tacks".

"They then expired with frightful pains
Inside their bowels, lungs and brains".

This new life of (evil) domesticity changes Miss Squill and her relationship with the world to a point where

"Her laugh made beetles swoon; her frown
Made geese and cows turn upside down".

Then one day the Devil returns.

"He seized her hair, and with his hoof
He kicked a way out through the roof".

"The end had come, and this was it;
He dropped her in the flaming pit".

(Gorey 1980)

On the last illustration, we see Miss Squill falling headfirst into the pit of flames, while Beëlphazoar watches, a look of shock and horror on its beaked face.

To me, *The Disrespectful Summons* tells a story of creative companionship in the wake of a traumatic experience. Miss Squill was struck down, to the point of receiving a mark on her chest, and Beëlphazoar appears in response to this wound. It helps Miss Squill create through cooking, needlework, and reading; sure, what they create are dreadful things, but I cannot help but appreciate this destructive creation and creative destruction in the wake of a wound. Beëlphazoar itself seems named after this duality, its name evoking the demonic "Beelzebub", connecting the familiar to Hell, but also "bezoar", a stone found in the stomach of both human and non-human animals, and which, according to folklore, works as an antidote to any poison. In this way, Beëlphazoar embodies a promise of potential healing through creative and domestic work, but a complicated healing, as Beëlphazoar stems from the same place – Hell – as the trauma itself.

There is something about Beëlphazoar that reminds me of Nigel, in that both are helpful yet slightly hellish companions seemingly stemming from a wound of sorts, which they try to manage on their human's behalf, not least during creative processes. When attempting to visualize Nigel, I see Beëlphazoar sitting on my shoulder, a shadowy silhouette with bat wings, horns, and big, round eyes, pointing at the screen with claw-like fingers. This comparison would indicate that the writer with a Nigel is a witch of sorts, or at least someone accused of witchcraft, which is perhaps not that far-fetched, considering the similarities between "spell" and "spelling" and how both are connected to an address, a reaching out, a calling upon something beyond the (human) self.

Snap, Bette Hund, Gielster, and Register

According to Etymonline, a familiar is a "demon, evil spirit that answers one's call",[1] suggesting that one of the primary characteristics of the familiar is that it first of all is called upon, summoned, conjured, and comes to be through a response to an address. Within the Western cultural imaginary, the familiar spirit is probably best known as the witch's black cat, though the familiar takes many shapes within European folklore as well as in the documentations available from the European witch trials between (approximately) 1485 and 1690 (Kallestrup 2009, 15). In broad, generalizing terms, the familiar of folklore and witch trials is typically a small devil, an imp, that has been summoned from Hell and, being capable of shapeshifting, has metamorphosed into the shape of an animal (such as black cats and toads). Looking to my own country, Denmark, the familiar is at times referred to as a *dreng* (roughly translated: [farm] boy/farm hand) or as a *hjælpedæmon* (helper demon) (Ejstrud and Christensen 2018, 46–47). The witch feeds her familiar her own blood in exchange for its help with her witchcraft. As is often the case with familiars in other European contexts, these creatures are related to pre-Christian helper creatures, such as *husånder* (spirits of the house), *gårdboer* (farm dwellers), and *nisser* (elves, fairies) (Ibid., 54). Examples of Danish familiars, or *drenge*, are:

Snap, who – in the shape of a rooster – leapt across Knud Poulsen while he was sleeping, causing his death. Snap was supposedly carrying out the orders of Anne Staffens, who, in 1620, was accused of witchcraft (Johansen 1991, 70).

Bette Hund (Wee Dog), who came to Inge Jensdatter from Melholt in 1624, when she, according to the accusations against her, denounced her Christian faith by blowing through the keyhole of Ulsted Church. Bette Hund, aptly named by Jensdatter, had taken the shape of a small, black, shaggy dog, and it greeted its new mistress by scratching her nose, thereby leaving the mark of the Devil on her face. Since then, Bette Hund followed Jensdatter everywhere (Ibid., 75).

And finally, *Gielster* and *Register*, the supposed helper devils of Sophie Kier and Appelonis, who were accused of witchcraft in the Danish town of Viborg in 1571 (Nielsen 2018). Little is known about the appearance of Gielster and Register, but their names indicate creatures that are noisy. Michael Lerche Nielsen explains that Gielster may derive from words such as *gælstre* and *gjæl*, all indicating loud noises, not least created by animals such as dogs and roosters. It may also be a reference to Galster, which, according to Nielsen, is synonymous with the word Zauber, German for "magic" (Nielsen 2018).

In this way, the name of Gielster indicates a barking, noisy creature. Register, on the other hand, is more straightforward, meaning a "register" or recipe, but it is also a slightly tongue-in-cheek description of an annoying person, not least a nosy woman. Nielsen suggests that "register", too, may be associated with sound in the form of *rumstere*: a noisy rummaging. In this way, both Gielster and Register evoke something noisy and more-than-human. But (potential) familiars do not only make sound, they are also excellent listeners, at least according to Thomas Aquinas' influential writings on magic and theology.

Aquinas explains that there are two kinds of miracles. The first is the kind bestowed by God and brought about by pious prayer that is not asking for anything for the individual but for help to further the work of God. The other kind is the one motivated by selfish needs (Kallestrup Nyholm 2009, 50). He goes on to explain that some users of magic may think that they are invoking the powers of God when they use magic to further their own causes, but the truth is that God does not grant selfish wishes – only the Devil and his demons do. In other words, when using magic to further your own interests, you have implicitly entered into a pact with the Devil, even if you did not intend to. This was also the case when applying magic in order to gain knowledge that was otherwise not intended for humans, for example, through the use of divination. When applying magic to ask "unnatural" questions, such as questions about the future, "it was only demons who would stoop to replying, and therefore the answers were always false" (Ibid., 50. Translated from Danish by me). And an answer, whether from God or demons, was necessary, because – according to Aquinas – the conjurer has no powers to make anything happen without the aid of either divine or diabolic forces:

> The force had to come from whomever or whatever the conjurer had addressed. Magical rituals were defined by the fact that the practitioner contacted something outside of human nature. He summoned a force that was superior to him – he summoned demons. . . . Thomas Aquinas concluded that magic was *only* possible through the aid of the Devil or demons. The conjurer's tools – not least words and incantations – possessed no powers in themselves. It was the Devil, who made the magical ritual effective.
>
> (Kallestrup 2009, 43. Translated from Danish by me, emphasis by Kallestrup)

According to this understanding of magic, the ritual becomes a means of address; the conjurer must address themselves through words ("spell-work" in more than one sense) to someone – or something – outside of human nature in order for the magic to be effective, and apparently, it is primarily demons who will listen. Within traditional demonology, the reasons for demons to listen are based in their attempts to trick human beings into apostasy and the damning of their souls, usually through deception and "false" miracles (Ibid., 43).

To me, however, there is a sense of generosity in this listening, in the answer to an address that stems not from a pious desire to serve God but from more earthly needs, so to say; from desires for wealth, love, and success as well as protection against pain and suffering.

I see some connections between the figure of the familiar and the Nigels of the world and their people; the editor-Nigel is also summoned through an address, a call, a plea, but this plea is silent, more a sense of hurt than a meaningful human voice and not necessarily intentional. When summoned, both editor and familiar attempt to aid their person in their spell(ing)-work, making it effectual; but they never do this from a purely innocent position, never not *from* the wound they are somehow trying to protect their person from. As such, I know my own Nigel will never fully succeed in protecting me from pain, and therefore, it will never go away, and since it will never go away, I am in some sort of pain from which it must protect me, and therefore, it cannot go away, etc. It is a strange relationship but one grounded in intimate knowledge of one another. I want to learn how to live with it, my editor-familiar, in a way that is bearable; how to create with it, how to read and write with it while it sits there on my shoulder, noisy as a rooster or a barking dog ("delete delete delete!"). I therefore turn to Gloria E. Anzaldúa, who knows what it is like attempting to create while in the company of the creatures of folklore – and with a wound.

The Wound

I had not initially planned to read chapter five of Anzaldúa's book *Light in the Dark* (2015) but came across it by chance when I was doing a ctrl+f search for something in the digital version of the book. I ended up in the company of la Llorona, as she wailed at Anzaldúa to start writing (Anzaldúa 2015, 96), and I stayed a bit, for I had no better place to be; at that point, I had been working on this chapter for close to two years, and my stomach dropped whenever I considered picking it back up. I needed help, and here was suddenly, unexpectedly, a conversation between Anzaldúa and a host of creatures from myth and folklore, all deeply involved in her creative process.

In *Light in the Dark*, Anzaldúa shows how she approaches writing through "archetypal cultural figures, welling up from el cenote, el fuente fecundo or pool in the personal and cultural unconscious formed by the waters of many rivers: the spiritual and the mundane, indigenous Mexican, Chicano, Basque, Spanish, Latino Euro-American, and cultures of color" (Ibid., 88). These creatures of folklore and spirituality, such as the ghostly la Llorona, haunt and aid Anzaldúa in her work (Ibid., 96), and in the first part of chapter 5, the collaboration with these archetypical figures and the forces associated with them run fairly smoothly. Then things begin to change; the deadline passes, and Anzaldúa – or the "you" of the chapter, which is written in the third person – is in the claws of "the demons who always try blocking you before the finish" (Ibid., 97). Reading this, I sat up a little straighter. At this point in the writing process, Anzaldúa struggles with her own inner critique, whom she some-times calls the ego and other times "the critical, editing voice" (Ibid., 104); a voice she must confuse and distract so the figure of la Llorona can take over and create through chaos, whereas the ego insists that chaos must be avoided and "that you write 'better'" (Ibid., 103). Even after she has completed a few drafts, the inner voice messes with her, and she starts worrying that the text she is working on is the worst she has ever done (Ibid., 110), and that she is a coward for not going far enough in her writing (Ibid., 112). She is blocked, and it is not until she goes for a walk and ends up right next to the depths of a sinkhole that she comes face to face with a possible solution (Ibid., 113). So how does one get unstuck? I leave her response here as it looked after I copied it from the digital version I was reading, all jumbled by the format-ting. It looks like a poem to me, an (unintentional) disturbance and change in perspective, which is exactly what I needed.

> To dismantle your block, you must change your behavior. To change your behavior,
> you must change your attitude. To change your atti-
> tude,
> you must change some basic beliefs about yourself, your writing habits, and your ability to do the work . . . .
> What notion about writing or about this stage in par-
> ticular is holding you up? That you should be able to whip out these historias faster? This is your monster – the
> myth that real writing
> comes out perfect in a few drafts.
> You know that to become unblocked something must give, some-
> thing
> must die – your
> ambition, your obsession with perfection. You
> have to let go of the illusion that the writer exerts full conscious con-
> trol over her writing process.
>
> (Anzaldúa 2015, 114)

In this moment, Nigel and I slip in and out of the "you". I can relate to the perfectionism, to the anxiety that what I do is not quick enough, not good enough, not relevant to anyone, and Nigel heeds the call and rushes to my side, ready to help me steer across the depths of a wound I am not ready to face. "You haven't checked Twitter in five minutes, let's have a look at that . . .", it says in one of its kinder moments. "How about Instagram? Oh yeah, some pics from your favourite vintage store, that's the stuff! Now maybe YouTube, let's have a look, it'll be quick . . ." I don't summon Nigel on purpose, but as a familiar, it does not need to be summoned consciously, it does not need a specific magic spell – it responds, I think, to my rising anxiety, to a call for a miracle that is not in service of a greater good but a need to get myself out of a situation where I am losing control, where I am about to plunge into an old wound. Nigel helps me avoid criticism through evasion or, paradoxically, through ramped-up criticism. It helps me steer clear of facing my own flaws and insecurities, which inevitably surface during the writing process. "To write is to expose yourself", writes Anzaldúa. "[T]o let down the protective walls – a given that comes with the territory. Today estas cansada; you're too tired to face your flawed criatura" (Anzaldúa 2015, 112).

Nigel seems a different creature from the ones that help Anzaldúa write; it is not the chaotic la Llorona but perhaps more related to the overly critical editor voice, which Anzaldúa must distract. But I am inspired by Anzaldúa working together with these "archetypal cultural figures", as she calls them, and

Figure 4.1 *Mad Meg*, 1563, Pieter I Bruegel. Pieter I Bruegel, Mad Meg, MMB.0045, Museum Mayer van den Bergh, image: Michel Wuyts.

Source: Courtesy of Museum Mayer van den Bergh.

how they help her in her work. By thinking of Nigel as Nigel, a named creature in its own right with ties to a European-Scandinavian folklore tradition – the world of *hjælpedjævle* such as Snap, Bette Hund, Gielster, and Register, and their people, Anne Staffens, Inge Jensdatter, Sophie Kier and Appelonis – perhaps I can change the affective relationship I have with it, make it not merely an editor but a creative companion as well. To do that, however, I need to consider what happens when Nigel is summoned and when it is at its most active, that is, when I am close to falling into a metaphorical sinkhole of that which is difficult, even painful to face. In the case of Miss Squill, she most definitely went headfirst into her wound, into her pit, her Hell (her text?), and Beëlphazoar watched in horror as it failed at its task of keeping this hole (text?) at bay. Yet it was the sinkhole that helped Anzaldúa, and according to her, the road out of the pit seems to go via giving up on attempting to fully control the writing process.

White Fish and Hellmouth

In the first part of this chapter, I wrote that Nigel and I revise stories to Hell and back, and the metaphor was not quite random, as I had Miss Squill's pit and Anzaldúa's sinkhole in mind. According to Rachel Falconer, Hell is "not only a concept and an imagined space-time; it is also a narrative". By this, she means that journeys through underworlds lend themselves as structuring metaphors for "experiences of suffering and transformation" (Falconer 2010, 217). This transformative aspect of Hell, "in which one accrues wisdom on the journey through experience 'at the limit'" (Ibid., 218), complicates the traditional understanding of Hell as a final, "evil" destination to be avoided at all costs. Instead, travels down into the depths of the world can be necessary and unavoidable as well as transformative, which reminds me of Anzaldúa's encounter with the sinkhole and other depths during the writing process. "Mapping the different terra incognitae with their shadowy indwellers enables you to evolve and grow", she writes. "[B]ut only after putting you through a crucible" [Anzaldúa 2015, 96]).

Apart from Miss Squill and Anzaldúa, I also had Mad Meg in mind. In Pieter Bruegel's painting *Mad Meg* (*Dulle Griet*, 1563), a tall woman leads a group of women to the mouth of Hell, where they plunder a village filled with demonic creatures. The painting is supposedly about the madness of Meg and her army of women and their foolish and greedy endeavour (Sullivan 2010, 116). I do, however, love the figure of Meg; her red nose, bulging eyes, clothes in disarray, and various rubbish and treasure falling from her hastily stuffed bag. She is about to dive headfirst into the mouth of Hell, she is about to go there willingly, and not in the service of God; on the contrary, *Mad Meg* is considered a possible "moral lesson, a warning against the sins of anger, avarice, gluttony, and lust" (Ibid., 125). This makes her an excellent potential guide for the likes of Miss Squill, still stuck in the flaming pit.

I brought some printouts of the *Mad Meg* painting to a writing session with Nina, Katja, and Marietta. The writing prompt was to find a creature in the image, a potential familiar, and write from their perspective. Nina chose a big white fish, Katja and Marietta chose the mouth of Hell, and I wrote from the perspective of a weird little creature found in the middle of the village. In the Alien Arrivals Intertext preluding this chapter, I have put the voices of these creatures together into a one-but-multiple creature, an idea sparked by Katja's text, where the mouth of Hell is interviewed ("Oh oh they interviewed the creature").

Returning to our writings on Mad Meg after (almost) having finished this chapter, I read them a little differently than I did the first time. Now, I read them as stories from the wound, from the depths mentioned by Anzaldúa, and as possible starting points for addressing what it means to be in the pits while writing, what kind of company one keeps there, and what one must give up in order to return to the surface – never unscathed and never not transformed ("they call it extinction and apocalypse – Hell. I call it breakfast", says Nina's white fish, gobbling up some poor man's leg). The Mad Meg writing prompt offered a way into and out of Hell, which created a Frankensteinian arrival text with a talking, devouring, many-mouthed beast made as much from play as from frustration and stuckness. "This was a very hard task", says Katja's Hell mouth. "And I have never had so much trouble writing". This mirrors many of my own writing experiences. Automatic writing, one of the methods we have worked with for this book, and which we used for the Mad Meg prompt, has been a means of sacrificing what must be sacrificed in order to write, that is, perfectionism and control. It is a way of distracting one's own editor demons, so one can go into the pits long enough to face one's writing and hopefully return again. But it is not a sure-fire method, and at times, our familiars will not be distracted. They know the pits, they come from the pits, and they are fearful of what you might find there.

Nigel

Nigel is on my shoulder again, whisper-barking-cawing that we should check out that YouTube-video and maybe refill the coffee that has gone cold. "Did you decide on buying those sandals you've been considering for weeks now? Let's have a look again", it says, claws hovering over my hand on the mouse.

This is the last bit of the chapter. We need to wrap it up, we need to start working on other parts of the book, and Nigel is getting antsy. I recognize this feeling. I know the little pressure points from its claws on the back of my neck, the knot in my stomach, the shallow breathing. We need to wrap this up, and Nigel is getting busy, there are a thousand things we could be doing instead of writing, and it is listing them all; I hardly realize I am back on Instagram before I click "like" on a friend's dog picture. "I should turn off the internet", I say, and Nigel agrees. "You should! Get up, go there, switch the button! And bring your phone back with you, just in case there's an urgent email or, you know, the sandals are on sale . . ."

"You've learned that writing about writing is more about life than it is about writing", Anzaldúa says. "[T]hat writing mirrors the struggle in your own life, from denial to recognition and change; that writing illumines your fears and dreams. All these insights are precious because you wrestled them out of the granite walls of your creative block" (Anzaldúa 2015, 115). I do not know exactly what I have wrestled from my writing block just yet, which makes me – and Nigel – unsure how to end this text. I do not know if our relationship has gotten any better from the venture into the pits, into the archetypes of European/Danish familiars. Perhaps this idea of "better" is what I need to let go of, at least if "better" is a stand-in for "perfect". "To get past this last wall, you must change your assumptions about what finishing means", Anzaldúa says. "Whenever you read any of your published work, you think it needs more revisions. There is never a final 'fin,' just a lot of small ones. You have to accept the imperfections of your work, accept its partial incoherence, accept the fact that it will never attain the surface of a water-smoothed stone. Like a person's life, all art is a work in progress" (Ibid., 115).

I know that co-writing and creative communities help me write, as has been the case with the alien writing I have done together with Nina, Katja, Marietta, and our figures (also with "Monster Writing"; see Henriksen et al. 2021). By working with the multiplicity inherent to all writing – what we refer to as the spectral collectivity of writing in this volume (see, for example, Prologue, this volume) – I experience a sense of support as well as encouragement to give up control to some extent and focus less on perfection and more on process. Naming my editor, not least naming it after another person's editor, has been a part of acknowledging and attempting to live with these multiple and more-than-human aspects of writing, as well as creating a sense of companionship over pure editorship. It has provided me with a language for speaking to others, inviting others into my writing anxieties and me into theirs, to co-create small, sometimes transient communities of people who also fear the writing-pits and live with a Nigel of their own from time to time. It becomes a source of fun; as Julia Cameron points out (France and Romolini 2023, 33:29–33:40), it is silly to have a small creature called Nigel sitting on your shoulder, nit-picking your work, being helpfully unhelpful. I imagine it as Beëlphazoar, same little shadowy familiar. I imagine it tucked into the foot of my bed at night. I imagine it following me around the kitchen as I make coffee, getting ready to write, listing off 92 Entirely Evil things to Do instead. "We could poison the neighbours", it says. "Turn geese and cows upside down? Make a fudge of pounded pencil-stubs and sludge!"

"What I'm saying is, we can always wrap this up tomorrow".

Note

1 Online Etymology Dictionary, s.v. "familiar (adj.)", accessed July 23, 2023, www.etymonline.com/word/familiar.

Figure 5.1 The Animals Noticed Us, and. Collage created for this publication based on photographs by the three authors of this volume.

5   More-than-Human Ethics and Poetics

Nina Lykke

In the previous chapters and Alien Arrivals texts (Intertexts I–III), six figures, three of them human, three of them more-than-human, have engaged
with each other in pairs, i.e. two by two. In this chapter, I will engage in a
cross-cutting reflection on the alien encounters which have been tried out,
imagined, and articulated in these chapters. My focus is the questions of ethics, aesthetics, and aesthesis (sensibilities) that these more-than-human meetings and conversations open. The reflections will be framed by a posthuman
phenomenological approach (Neimanis 2017; Lykke 2022) and through contemplations of posthuman poetics (Lykke 2022). Moreover, I will build on
the assumption that we (humans and other-than-humans alike) are all part of
a planetary kinship which we should pay respect to and consider in a bio- and
geoegalitarian perspective, that is: as (modern) humans, we should unlearn
our ideas about human exceptionalism and try to relearn to see ourselves as
part of a planetary collective of myriads of biological and geological, organic
and inorganic beings who are equally entitled to care and respect.

Posthuman phenomenology is a framework for analyzing subjective experiences that are shared across species due to our embodied kinship as planetary beings as well as a tool for better understanding differences which also
need to be respected in cross-species companionship relations. To establish
alien encounters on ethical grounds that respect the bio- and geoegalitarian
planetary kinship, of which we are part, we need to take into account both
what we share across the more-than-human world and what makes us differ.
As a human being, I am not a tree. In contrast to the tree, my body is not bound
to a specific place through a root but crafted to move around. However, even
though the tree and I, among others in terms of mobility, are in existentially
different situations, we still share many kinds of embodiment. For example,
both of us are mortal beings and dependent on water, light, air, and Earth's
gravity, albeit in different ways. Together with artistic-poetic ways of working
such as the posthuman poetics to which we commit in this book, posthuman
phenomenology is important as a tool for teasing out, on an experiential level,
the network of embodied similarities and differences that make up our ancestral planetary kinship.

DOI: 10.4324/9781003373766-8

This is a kinship that, for centuries, has been neglected due to the episte-mologies of ignorance, which Euromodern science and philosophy, together with Judeo-Christian dualist thought, have established through the construc-tion of a sharp dividing line between Human and Nonhuman. This is a divid-ing line, which Derrida aptly characterized as an "abyss" (2008), so, indeed, its undoing is not a quick fix. When considering the destructive effects of the divide and their overcoming, it is also important to note that the divide is not only discursive. Its power is structurally reinforced through racialized and (post)colonial capitalism and its institutionalized power differentials between the sovereign modern (white, "civilized", heteropatriarchal) subject, Univer-sal Man (Lykke 2018), and His thingified world of others; that is: the world considered as Universal Man's reservoir of resources for wealth-creation, defined through de-, in-, and non-humanization of people, lands, animals, plants, and minerals (Yusoff 2018), as well as through a total neglect of the tricksterous processes of spiritmattering which Indigenous philosophies ask us to pay careful attention to (Anzaldúa 2015; Schaeffer 2018).

As indicated in the introduction and spelled out through our three alien figures, slugs, diatoms, and familiars, the focus of this volume is the animal, plant, and mineral part of this thingification as well as the neglect of spirit-mattering trickstery. In this context, we claim that an important dimension of undoing and unlearning the sovereign human subject's modes of acting vis-à-vis the thingified worlds of animals, plants, other organisms, and inor-ganic matter as well as its exorcizing the worlds of ghosts and spirits from its domain is to recognize our planetary kinship with all these worlds of others on a deep corpo-affective level. Only through undoing and unlearning the epistemologies of ignorance and the multilayered *in*sensitivities, which are correlates of the thingification and so ingrained in the bodies and sensuous apparatus of Euromodern humans, can other alternative collaborative prac-tices be enabled. We consider ways of working which cut across modes of philosophical reflection and artistic/poetic articulation of more-than-human kinship as pathways to unlearn and relearn while trying to ensure that the relearning will be anchored in both an intellectual and a corpo-affective sense.

In this chapter, I will contemplate our three stories of encounters with slugs, diatoms, and familiars with posthuman phenomenology and more-than-human poetics as lens. However, firstly, in order to set the tone for the chapter's contemplations, I start with a poem, "And the Animals Noticed Us". I wrote this poem on a writing retreat on Fur together with Katja – the one where she was bitten by a slug, as she describes in Chapter 2, this volume. Secondly, I reflect upon the meanings of "alienness" that we draw on in our three stories. I contemplate the ways in which we use the term "alien" to avoid the dual trap of anthropomorphization and denial of any kind of common ground between humans and "aliens". I discuss the pathways we take towards steering clear of both sides of this trap in our processes of alien co-becomings and engaging in alien companionships. Thirdly, I focus on the alien arrivals to the human interlocutors' world. What does it mean that the alien figures in all three stories came unexpected and uninvited into the worlds of the three humans and that the encounters materialized in situations where the human subjects, for different reasons, were in vulnerable situations? Fourthly, I consider the planetary ethics of alien companionship, which, based on embodied recognition of planetwide kinship relations, came into our horizons through the processes of more-than-human co-becoming and becoming-other in which we engaged together with the alien figures. In the last section, I return to the poem "And the Animals Noticed Us" to discuss its poetic articulation of the ethics of alien companionship that we argue for and the posthuman poetics from which it emerged.

And the Animals Noticed Us!

1.

A deer, a fox, a crab and a wasp
noticed our presence
on the island.
The dear and the fox
stood still for a long, long time,
looked vigilant at us,
as if congealed,
arrested in their forward movement.
They observed us carefully,
oh so carefully.
What did they see, smell, feel,
when they saw us?
The crab and the wasp
did not just watch us,
but tried to touch you.
The crab perhaps defended
its quiet space
which you disturbed
while walking in the shallow water
to do underwater filming,
where strange diatomaceous tentacles
stretch out from cliff to seabed.
The wasp flew towards you several times,
neglecting me,
even though we sat
next to each other
at the garden table.
Why was it so bent on you?

When Earth Others
take something from you,
give it back.[1]

2.

You invited a slug,
a big brown critter,
to slide over your hand,
lovingly or hungrily,
or perhaps in quite a different mood,
unknown to humans.
It moved along your index finger.
You compared it to a cat's tongue.
I prepared myself to offer it my finger, too.
But when it reached your cuticle,
it bit you,
thrilled by the soft spot,
it felt that you had there.
Blood came out.
You ran inside the cottage
to clean the wound
with disinfectant.
I offered the slug
a cherry and
a boiled egg.
Abjecting,
atoning,
attuning?
You took a picture
of the egg,
congealed in the moment
when it flew through the air,
before landing in the bushes,
where the slug seemed to live.

When Earth Others
take something from you,
give it back.

3.

While I was walking
in the wet grass

on the top of the diatomaceous cliffs
after the big thunder shower,
convinced that this place was safe,
four ticks pierced my skin,
two in the groin,
one on the stomach,
and one on the backside of my knee.
I have never before encountered ticks here,
even though I have walked on these paths
so many times
since we scattered my beloved's ashes
in the diatom-rich waters
outside of the cliffs
eight years ago.
These cliffs are my place of worship,
the site where, desiring,
I anticipate my ashes
going to the waterworld
and staying there forever . . .
Now the four ticks made me aware
that there are more things going on
in this alien world
than I imagined.
They sucked my blood.
Did they enjoy the taste?
One of them stayed on my body for a whole week.
But I tore them out,
all four of them.
One by one.
I flushed their tiny bodies
in the toilet.
Shaken by this unprepared
alien encounter,
I even considered
to get a vaccination
to immunize my vulnerable human body
against tickborne encephalitis,
Ticks are resilient.
I wonder,
if the four ticks
survived my violent attempt to kill them.

When Earth Others
take something from you,
give it back.

4.

When I came home
after the visit to the island,
tiny little ants one day
ran around on my living room floor.
Had they taken a ride
on my travelling bags?
Had I unknowingly,
through my insensitive human behaviour,
forced these little critters
to migrate from their
cosy forest home
to my urban house,
where food supplies
perhaps are scarce?

When Earth Others
take something from you,
give it back.

What Is "an Alien"? Traps of Anthropomorphizing or Denying Common Ground

In the introductory chapter (1), we referred to feminist reclaimings of the terms "alien" and "alien encounter". Now I will take a look at the specific ways in which these reclaimings work in our stories and discuss more specifically what the term "alien" is meant to do in the context of our stories and analyses. What does it mean to speak of our meetings with slugs, diatoms, and familiars as *alien* encounters?

We (the human co-authors) chose the terms "alien" and "alien encounter" as framework for this book to indicate our will to navigate between two major traps when it comes to attempts to rethink more-than-human relationships and learn from other-than-human perspectives. These two traps are anthropomorphization, on the one hand, and denying any possibility for bridging the abyss between Human and Earth Others, on the other hand. While anthropomorphizing erases significant existential differences, the denial of any common ground ends up as just one more confirmation of the abyss and implicitly as a mere reproduction of human exceptionalism. With the designation "alien", we aim to steer clear of both these traps. We want to make sure that we do not gloss over our other-than-human companions' differences from us (humans) while, at the same time, recognizing that we share common ground with them insofar as all of us are critters of this planet. That the recognition of common ground should be part of our definition of "the alien" resonates with our reclaiming of feminist science fiction as described in the introduction. By

Figure 5.2 When Earth Others Take Something from You, Give It Back . . . Documentation of giving-back ritual, offering a boiled egg to the slug who bit Katja, Fur, Denmark.

Source: ©Katja Aglert and Nina Lykke

contrast to the kind of conventional sci-fi that just reproduces colonial images of conquest and submission, the traditions of feminist, anti-racist, and eco-critical sci-fi to which our work is indebted are to be understood as platforms for critiquing the here-and-now world on this planet. This means that the con-juring up of "alien" worlds should be plausible as critique of unjust social and ecological relations as they are in the here-and-now.

It is our aim to establish symphysizing companionships with the other-than-human aliens whom we encountered. Along the lines of Haraway, we understand such a companionship as built on deep-seated response-ability, the ability to respond in a situated, sensitive, and ethically responsible way (2008, 88–89). However, to this we add the notion of symphysizing (Lykke 2022, Forthcoming a, d), an ability to corpo-affectively empathize, co-sense, and co-experience – with due recognition of existential differences in a both corpo-affective and cognitive sense. We want to establish committing rela-tionships with the alien figures but without assimilating their experiences and perspectives into a universalized, humanocentric mode of perceiving, or, con-versely, without totally giving up upon the question of shared grounds. This means that we need to make serious efforts to respectfully symphysize with them but also that we seriously must speculate about potential similarities and differences in their ways of experiencing, perceiving, and unfolding perspec-tives on the world.

What similarities are concerned, posthuman phenomenology that looks into the ways in which our common belonging to the planetary body link Earth inhabitants to certain conditions (such as, for example, being depend-ent on water, light, air, and a certain kind of gravity), provides entry points for our speculations on modes of establishing symphysizing companion-ship. Humans, slugs, and diatoms are all mortal beings, and, albeit in dif-ferent ways, dependent on water, light, air, and the gravity that characterize Earth. Differences, too, can be contemplated with a posthuman phenom-enology as framework. As noted by Katja (Chapter 2, this volume), in a posthuman phenomenological sense, a major difference between slugs' and humans' mode of perceiving the world is that the former, first of all, get to know their surroundings through smell and touch, whereas they do neither see them very well nor hear them, as do humans. Confronted with the ques-tion of similarities and differences in my diatom companions' ways of expe-riencing the world, I have, for example, used posthuman phenomenological thought to speculate in depth about their plant-like aspects. The fact that they are photosynthesizing creatures makes their bodily relation to oxygen and nitrogen significantly different from mine. Even though these micro-algae are still aerobic, that is, dependent on oxygenated surroundings, and, therefore, likely to die under anoxic conditions, their experience of dying due to lack of oxygen will be different from the kind of death by suffoca-tion which humans and fish will suffer when deprived of oxygen (Lykke Forthcoming a).

These examples indicate that posthuman phenomenology can be a good tool to contemplate experiential-level similarities and differences between humans, slugs, and diatoms. But can we also use a posthuman phenomenological approach to try to symphysize with the perspective of familiars, who evidently evade the categorizations as scientifically describable entities that the phenomenological understanding of slugs and diatoms still rely on? Yes, I argue, if we combine the analysis with a Derridean hauntology (1994) and, moreover, with a decolonial thinking along the lines of a pluriversal approach (de la Cadena and Blaser 2018). Such a thinking is built on a pluritopic hermeneutics (Tlostanova and Mignolo 2009, 2012). This means that Western and indigenous philosophies and cosm-ontologies are both taken into account, while Western interpretations, claiming universality, are critically deuniversalized. Against these backgrounds, I claim that a posthuman phenomenology of familiars is possible. Within the framework of a Derridean hauntology, familiars can be likened to ghosts and spectres – i.e., ephemeral beings with a phenomenal existence. Seen from a pluriversal perspective, familiars bear resemblance to spirit helpers in indigenous philosophies (Anzaldúa 2015; Schaeffer 2018). Familiars can be seen as belonging to the big mass of spirited beings of a-modern cosm-ontologies which people all over the planet (Europe included) have cultivated for thousands and thousands of years and which, in some contexts, have survived until this day, even though imperial and colonial projects and territorial claims, based on powerful world religions (not the least Christianity), have tried to force them into other (hierarchical) ways of perceiving and approaching the world. The European witch hunts, through which knowledge of familiars, as Line pinpoints (Chapter 4, this volume), were recorded as part of the legal protocols used to condemn the witches to be burnt at the stake, are examples of the violent reinforcing of new universalizing epistemes and sense regimes; they indicate that there are certain similarities between the processes of eradication of ancient knowledges in Europe and in the colonies in early modernity – both reinforced with the Christian church as facilitator.

Against the background of this kind of Derridean as well as pluritopic rethinking, I argue that it is possible to draw posthuman phenomenological approaches into the speculations about the possibilities for establishing ethically sound, seriously symphysizing companionships not only with slugs and diatoms but also with familiars. Though, in this case, too, I find it important to keep the mentioned dual trap in mind, which implies that we should try to avoid both anthropomorphization and approaches that imply a denial of common ground. However, it seems as if both the Derridean approaches to ghosts (1994) and indigenous interpretations of spirit helpers (Anzaldúa 2015; Schaeffer 2018) are very helpful also in this sense. In both contexts, these ephemeral critters are, indeed, already closely associated with phenomena which are defined along the lines of our dual definition of an "alien" companion – as a figure who is not to be anthropomorphized but still considered as one with whom humans share common ground. Beëlphazoar, Nigel, and the historical witches' familiars who appear in Line's story (Chapter 4, this volume) are all other-than-human, but they also share a lot of common ground with "their" humans, Miss Squill, Line, etc. This, I argue, opens horizons for contemplating companionships through posthuman phenomenology, also when it comes to familiars and their ephemeral in-betweenness.

Encountering the Alien: Vulnerability and Unexpectedness

Having established the meaning of the term "alien" in our stories, I shall now dig more into the storylines and start to contemplate the initial encounters with slugs, diatoms, and familiars. How did each of the three humans become entangled in alien encounters in the first place? When reflecting upon our encounters with slugs, diatoms, and familiars (Chapters 2, 3, and 4, this volume), it is noteworthy that none of the three humans chose our alien interlocutor. They entered our lives without being anticipated or prepared for. Katja's slug project started because her garden was "invaded" by slugs, and it seemed to her as if her house would be "invaded", too, if she did not do something about it, and from her mixed feelings and first impulse to kill the "invaders", a long-term artistic relationship developed. I myself came unexpectedly to the amazing world of diatoms as part of my mourning practices and became immensely attracted to these critters while extending my spiritmattering and symphysizing companionship with my dead partner's ashes to the diatomite and watery assemblages with which it had become part. Line stumbled upon familiars through the text and images of US writer Edward Gorey's poem "The Disrespectful Summons" (1980). The poem made her angry because of the unjust treatment of Miss Squill. But it also introduced her to the fascinating bird-like creature Beëlphazoar, who ironically subverted the scientific world view's relegation of monstrous beings such as familiars to the world of irrational superstition while establishing a joyful, attractive, and intimate cohabitation and companionship with Miss Squill.

A striking similarity between the otherwise different stories is the totally unplanned, uncontrolled, and unexpected character of the human subjects' first encounter with the alien. The arrival of the slugs, diatoms, and familiars to the world of the three humans happens out of the blue – totally unanticipated by the humans. Added to this, it is also important to note that the encounters, in all three cases, are related to a vulnerable situation for the human subject, who is pushed decisively outside of her comfort zones by the encounter or who is already for other reasons beyond this. Katja experienced the slug "invasion", as did many Scandinavians at the time, as the ultimately abject powers of horror. According to French psycholinguist Julia Kristeva (1982), abjection happens when any protective layer of symbolic representation breaks down, and the subject is left with strong and uncontrollable bodily responses of disgust. Such an abjection is what pushed Katja totally out of her comfort zones. For me, the meeting with diatoms was totally intertwined with my feelings of utter devastation after the loss of my lesbian life partner and my strong desires for love-death and becoming-one with the remains of my beloved and their new assemblages – the diatomite seabed and cliffs at Fur. When I met the diatoms, I was thus already totally beyond my comfort zones due to my grief. For Line, the process of academic writing has for years pushed her out of her comfort zones, making her vulnerable vis-à-vis obligations to write which are unavoidable in her academic profession. Caught in the tricky dilemmas which this situation keep producing for Line, she first encountered Beëlphazoar and Miss Squill and was later approached by the monstrous writing companion and editor, Nigel.

In addition to the unexpected arrival of slugs, diatoms, and familiars in our respective kinds of human worlds and our encountering them in situations of vulnerability, it is, moreover, significant for our three stories that the more-than-human relationships that have come into being through the alien encounters have been both generative and troubling. On the one hand, they have seriously prompted us to question human exceptionalism and exclusive sovereignty. However, on the other hand, starting to in-depth question and disrupt the epistemic habits which uphold human exceptionalism and their corpo-affectively ingrained correlates of *in*sensitivities towards the more-than-human world is no simple and easy one-way road. So the accounts of our alien encounters touch upon obstacles and negative experiences as well. Here, it is, of course, important to note that the relations between generativity and negativity/obstacles are complex and that negative experiences can be as generative as positive ones. So let me consider these complexities of our alien encounters in a bit more detail.

The slug-bite in Katja's story and her reflections on what it does to her human self to become-slug food show how difficult it is to unlearn the epistemic habits and sensibilities of the (Euromodern) sovereign human subject. The sovereign subject considers its entitlement to treat all other Earth inhabitants as plain food as indisputable but becomes utterly shocked when critters such as Katja's slug or the four ticks who (as described in my poem "And the Animals Noticed Us") bit me, take steps to turn this food-chain upside down. In my story about becoming a diatom advocate, it is significant that I came to my queer, more-than-human desire to co-become with the diatoms through my very human love for my lesbian life partner and that my posthuman process of co-becoming with diatoms unfolded from a story of human mourning. Finally, Line's story makes it clear how intimate bonds between witches and familiars have been outlawed by Christian morality based on contempt for the monstrous fleshiness of mundane needs as well as by modern science's distinctions between natural and supernatural, real and unreal. Moreover, the familiar does not necessarily act as a docile and purely helpful companion.

Still, in spite of or sometimes rather because of the troubles, our stories articulate lived experiences of efforts to make the alien encounters that came to us unexpectedly lead to generative companionships. They show how the encounters have helped us to engage in unlearning of epistemic habits of human exceptionalist thought, undoing of insensitive approaches to the more-than-human world, and opening up to processes of respectful and non-exploitative co-becoming.

Against the background of the overall similarities between our three stories, I suggest that the generativity of our alien encounters is perhaps, first of all, made possible by our vulnerabilities and by our willingness to immerse ourselves in unexpected events beyond our comfort zones. Important is also, I guess, that for all three of us (humans), it was existentially impossible to withdraw from the encounter. In states of abjection, deep mourning, or writer's block, the subject is not in control. In my recent book on death and mourning (Lykke 2022), I have teased out how, phenomenologically speaking, the mourning "I" has a distinctly better access to understand death than the sovereign "I". I argue that the latter will always resist the thought of death as the ultimate loss of control, whereas the mourning "I" might make friends with death as a way to become one with the dead beloved. Extending this argument to openly vulnerable or wounded subjects who come to engage in alien encounters, I argue that these subjects, too, in phenomenological terms, can perhaps experience, understand, and let themselves be touched by such encounters in more open-ended ways than the sovereign subject who, first of all, will focus on the traumatic loss of control. The subject position of the vulnerable human "I" is then, I suggest, to be considered as that which has made the generative aspects of our encounters possible and opened for this book's speculations about becoming epistemologically and sensuously other through alien guidance.

A Planetary Ethics of Alien Companionship

Besides the unexpectedness of our initial alien encounters, it is also to be noted that they all resulted in the eventual establishment of symphysizing companionships (Lykke 2022). They could have been one-time events. But instead, all of them became generative and unfurled as long-term commitments on the part of the humans. In different ways, we (the humans) have become advocates for slugs, diatoms, and familiars, and our engagements in these relations have led us to argue for a planetary ethics of alien companionship. I shall now unpack what we mean when we argue for such an ethics.

To define such an ethics, we build on what we already said about the individual companionships that we wanted to develop with our three alien figures – involving response-ability as well as a respectfully symphysizing and caring mode of approaching both differences and similarities between the companions. However, we also follow Haraway in her extension of the companionship concept from individual human/other-than-human relations (her mutually transformative, embodied relations to her dogs (2008)) to a planetary-scale sympoiesis (2016). As defined by Haraway (2016, 58–99), sympoiesis refers to a principle of co-evolving, which she sees as characteristic for all organisms. Sympoiesis is different from autopoiesis, self-organizing, in the sense that the former implies that organisms do not evolve in isolation but in interdependency. While Haraway from the start theorized human–dog companionship to critically disrupt human exceptionalism which reduced animals, *in casu* dogs, to mere stimulus-response machines, her reflection on sympoiesis extends the notion of companionship to more-than-human planetary relations as such. She reflects on the planet as a big network of sympoietic co-evolving organisms which it is urgent to attune to rather than continue to believe in human sovereignty and (mis)treat the planet against this backdrop. We take the point from Haraway that when the ability of all organisms to co-evolve sympoietically is scaled out to and seen in a planetary perspective, it implies that even small acts of attunement through symphysizing companionships, as we have described them in this book, come to stand as ways of acting ethically response-able which link individual micro-levels and overall planetary perspectives. We also note that it takes the question of an ethics of response-ability far beyond the humanist discussions in which it is often embedded (e.g., Walter 2014). Haraway's interpellation of planetary sympoiesis, response-ability, ethics, more-than-human companionship, and kinship disrupt any humanist framing.

Figure 5.3 A Sympoietic "Memory by an Orchid for Its Extinct Bee" (Haraway 2016, 69). Photograph of *Ophrys apifera* at Kew Gardens, commonly known as "Bee Orchid", June 2010. Photo: Andrew McRobb.

Source: © The Board of Trustees of the Royal Botanic Gardens, Kew.

Though, while paying tribute to these inspirations from Haraway, we shall also note that the planetary ethics of alien companionship, which our encounters with slugs, diatoms, and familiars have made us come to see as urgently needed in these times of ecological unbalances and disasters, is also, to some extent, transgressing the frameworks of *Staying with the Trouble* (2016), which, first and foremost, speaks about sympoiesis, kinship, and companionship between biological beings. First of all, through my relation with diatoms, which include diatomite and diatomaceous earth made of sediments of fossilized diatoms, we extend the planetary companionship networks to the world of geological formations. In so doing, we align our ontologizing with indigenous philosophy as well as with posthumanist scholars such as Bennett (2010) and Povinelli (2016) and decolonial scholars such as de la Cadena (2015) and Yusoff (2018). These are all scholars who, in different ways, have argued that the world of geological formations needs to be included in the framing of alter-ontologies. Secondly, through Line's companionship with familiars, we include forms of being in the companionship networks which are counted as not-real by Western rationality. As I argued in relation to the question of a posthuman phenomenology of familiars, this further extension of what our alter-ontologies encompass makes perfect sense with reference to a Derridean and a pluritopic hermeneutics. But, in addition, it is also possible to link directly back to Haraway here. To her account of the sympoietic relations which make up the world, she adds in passing the notion of symanimagenesis. Symanimagenesis refers to a self-organized co-evolving, implying mutual help at spiritual/animist levels (Haraway 2016, 88). Even though Haraway does not elaborate it further, I suggest that symanimagenesis and sympoiesis should be seen as intertwined (Schaeffer 2018, 1014; Lykke 2022) and that more-than-human planetary companionship and response-ability, therefore, should be understood as framed by both these ways of co-evolving and co-becoming. When Haraway, moreover, defines "companion species" as "less a category than a pointer to an ongoing 'becoming with'" (2008, 16), that is, to a shared process of mutual becoming across species and other borders, I assemble all these reflections in order to, finally, define an ethics of alien companionship as requiring an alignment with planetary processes of intertwined sympoiesis and symanimagenesis across borders between species, between organic and inorganic beings, as well as between molar entities and more ephemeral, spectral, and molecularized existences.

I see our stories of the ways in which the unexpected and unplanned alien encounters have unfurled and, for all three humans, keep involving efforts to co-become and try to become other together with slugs, diatoms, and familiars as attempts to materialize a planetary ethics of alien companionship. A main point in our stories is the sharpening of our sense-abilities, our abilities to symphysize with alien others (Treusch 2017; Lykke 2022), and, against this background, start to learn to become more and otherwise response-able and sensitive. Our alien encounters have become generative in this sense, too. But, again, let us underline that this does not mean that our efforts to co-become are or have always been successful. To live and materialize an ethics of alien companionship is not a tick-box but daily work to undo human exceptionalism and insensitivity towards the more-than-human world. It is about constantly trying to show response-ability and enhance one's more-than-human sense-ability in a perspective which is planetary and macropolitical in terms struggling for overall social and ecological justice, but also related to small-scale everyday-like mundane practices such as offering a finger to a slug, swimming with diatoms or writing with familiars. Anzaldúa (2015) underlines both the hard work and the everyday-like character of efforts to generate this kind of inner and outer change. She talks about such work as spiritual activism (2015, 89–90) when describing her long-term efforts to learn shamanistic skills and practices in alignment with her Aztec ancestors – to be used in political work towards social and ecological justice in the contemporary world. We suggest that efforts to materialize a planetary ethics of alien companionship, in similar ways, can be considered as a kind of continuous spiritual activism for social and ecological justice-to-come.

Posthuman Poetics

To emphasize the aesthetic implications of the outlined ethics of alien companionship, I shall end this chapter with a reflection on posthuman poetics and how it can work in tandem with philosophy. In so doing, I will return to my poem "And the Animals Noticed Us".

The poem makes the human "us" into an object of the animal gaze. In this way, the text poetically disrupts the subject position of the exceptional and sovereign, human "I" who is embodying the *hubris* of the zero-point (Castro-Gómez 2021), that is: the sovereign gaze, who is meant to observe without being an object of observation itself. In the poem, the subject–object relations are turned around, insofar as the animals are positioned as bearers of the "gaze" (or rather of the power to "notice", which includes other ways than seeing, since not all the animals use eyes as their primary organ of sensing and establishing perspectives on the world). Insofar as this is a poem written in human language by a human poet (me), this turning subject–object relations around is, of course, not to be considered as powerful enough to change relations outside of the poetic world of words. But within the framework of a posthuman poetics, the poem is nonetheless meant to question and trouble the notion of the objectifying, sovereign human gaze and make the point that other-than-humans have their own perspectives: they "look" back, they are response-able and not mere stimulus-response-machines.

This poem contemplates what it does to "us", modern humans, when the subject–object relation is turned around and considers how it forces us out of our comfort zones when changes in the hierarchical relation have threatening and troubling effects for our bodily well-being and integrity, such as the traumatic "becoming-prey" effect which Katja's story of the slug bite (Chapter 2, this volume) and Plumwood's account of the crocodile attack (Plumwood and Shannon 2012) capture so well. However, as Haraway as well as our stories of encounters with slugs, diatoms, and familiars suggest, an ethics of more-than-human companionship means that we as humans should do our best to "stay with the trouble" (2016).

To make this point forcefully, the poem's refrain is a remake of the main title of Danish writer Naja Marie Aidt's award winning poetic-autofictional novel about the traumatic death of her 25-year-old son (Aidt 2019). The main title of the novel is an oxymoron: *When Death Takes Something from You, Give It Back.* The oxymoron is a literary trope that is built on an apparent contradiction while, at the same time, articulating a paradox, which questions and perhaps challenges the opposition between the allegedly contradictory elements. With her highly complex and poetic oxymoron, Aidt challenges conventional oppositions between giving/taking and life/death. In my recycled version of the oxymoron, the lyrical "I" of "And the Animals Noticed Us" likewise challenges the opposition of giving/taking, although not in relation to the conventional opposition between life and death but to another abysmal divide – the one which Judeo-Christianity and Euromodern philosophy constructed between humans and all other inhabitants of the planet, the "Earth Others" (Plumwood 1993). As I read Aidt's title and text, the "I" of the novel encourages/advises/exhorts the bereaved "you" (an alter ego of the mourning "I") to rethink the opposition between life and death, insisting that the "you" should not just curse death as an enemy which bereaved her but instead consider the gifts to bring to the world of the dead as part of efforts to unfurl an ongoing and generative relationship between life and death, between the world of the living and that of the dead.

In resonance with this interpretation of Aidt's title and text, the lyrical "I" of my poem encourages/advises/exhorts the "you" (the alter ego of the human "I" whose feelings of bereavement stem from the loss of control and exceptional entitlement to sovereignty, occurring when Earth Others turn the subject–object relation around) to rethink the troubled Human/Earth Others relationship. The "you" should not just curse the loss of control and the lack of sovereign powers, revealed when Earth Others turn the subject–object relationship around, but instead consider the gifts to bring to the world of Earth Others while unfurling an ongoing and generative more-than-human companionship beyond the abysmal divide.

The poem and the oxymoronic poetic refrain are ways of showing rather than philosophically telling, what a planetary ethics of alien companionship is about. Show-don't-tell is a literary technique which aims at "showing" through images rather than "telling" through concepts and explanations:

When Earth Others
take something from you,
give it back.

Note

1 The refrain is a twisted recycling of the main title of Danish writer Naja Marie Aidt's autofictional-poetic novel *When Death Takes Something from You, Give it Back – Carl's Book* (Aidt 2019). The term "Earth Others" refers to Australian ecofeminist philosopher Val Plumwood, who coined this term (Plumwood 1993) as part of her eco-philosophical and intersectional analysis, which theorized the asymmetrical power relation between the human and the planet's other-than-human others in line with class oppression, sexism, racism, and colonialism.

Figure 6.1 Exquisite Corpse. Collage created for this publication based on photographs by the three authors of this volume. © Katja Aglert 2023.

6 Conversations on Alien Methods and Writing

Katja Aglert and Line Henriksen

This chapter is based on three conversations between the co-authors of this volume and edited by Katja and Line. The first conversation between Katja and Line prompted the second conversation, in which Line and Katja interview Nina, which prompted the third and final conversation between Katja and Line. The three-part structure was not planned from the start but grew from the various conversations we had on the topic of method and writing. In this way, the chapter (unintentionally) mirrors the triquetra that, in many ways, structures this book (Prologue, this volume), but it also – in a way – enacts the emergent methodologies (Lykke 2022, 20) behind the book, meaning that our methods have developed from the process itself rather than functioning as pre-planned itineraries. This methods chapter is therefore more of a retrospective reflection on the vulnerabilities, difficulties and joys that made us write the book in the ways we did than an explanation of the routes we deliberately took in our engagements with the alien figures. This retrospective nature of the methods chapter is also why it is situated here, towards the end of the book.

Troubled Writing

Katja's Studio
Stockholm, Sweden
May 2023
Katja and Line

Katja: Okay, it's recording.
Line: So, we wanted to talk about what kind of methods we have been using for the book, with a particular emphasis on automatic writing, and also the method of the methods chapter, that is, how we wrote this chapter. Maybe we should just jump right into the whole thing and eventually move onto some of the more nerdy aspects of how we understand methods as we go. Is there something I am forgetting?

DOI: 10.4324/9781003373766-9

Katja: No, I don't think so. I wonder if we should start with the reason why we are recording this conversation? One of the methods we have used during the work with the alien encounters is having conversations and recording those conversations as part of our explorations in order for them to potentially become material for this book.

Line: Yeah, and a bit of an archive for our thoughts, because we realized we forgot a lot of stuff. The alien encounters work began all the way back in 2016, so a lot of things have happened, and we started to record online meetings and use a recorder during face-to-face meetings. Now we are going to try and use this method as a means of writing this chapter on methods.

Katja: Exactly. Another reason we are doing it in this particular way is because we both found it difficult writing this chapter in a "properly academic" way.

Line: Yes, we were initially planning it as a more traditional methods chapter, which seemed perhaps not completely true to the project. At the same time, from a personal perspective, I have been having some trouble writing for months now, which is something I cover in my own chapter on writing with familiars (Chapter 4, this volume), so sitting down trying to write this methods chapter just ended up in procrastination for me. So, to stay true to the overall tone and aim of the alien encounters project, as well as attempt to write while in a bit of a block, we are sitting down for a chat. Our hope is to tell a part of the story of how we have been working with our alien figures and to consider if there is a method in there or multiple methods or something we can put in a toolbox and perhaps hand over to other people in case they want to do something similar to what we have been doing or wish to develop it further, taking it in different directions.

Katja: For me, at the heart of this project is the fact that we come from different disciplinary backgrounds in arts and academia, and that this prompts questions in relation to how we write the book so that it articulates and materializes a diversity of voices and perspectives. To record the conversations, in other words taking them seriously as research material, is something that has been encouraged by Nina, who has been working with conversation as a method in much of her current and past work (Hazekamp and Lykke 2022; Lykke 2022). Conversation has also been part of my work since 1999, when I tried it for the first time while doing research for an art project. In our own "alien encounters" project, conversation became a crucial tool of processing for me after the slug bite, which I experienced last year on the island Fur together with Nina (described in Chapter 2, this volume). She suggested that we should do a recording as soon as possible after the "bite event", and here, she asked me some questions in order for me to catch some of the immediate thoughts and feelings triggered by the experience. The conversation became such an important record for me to think together with as part of the writing of my slug chapter (Chapter 2, this volume), as well as a way to understand more about my own processual learning together with slugs through bodily multi-sensorial experiences.

Line: Can I ask you what you associate method or methodology with? What's your relationship to it as an artist?

Katja: For me, the word "method" translates to the way we do things when we do them repeatedly.

Line: All right, so there is a sense of repetition?

Katja: That's the way that I have come to understand it, though now when you comment on it, maybe it's more about how the idea of a method comes from the ability to tell someone else about how you have done something. For me, the way I work in my artistic practice, I don't begin by deciding about a method but rather just begin in a more open-ended manner. Only in retrospect, by reflecting on the work that has been done, it is possible to discern if there is a method to be teased out. This is very similar to how Nina describes emergent methodologies (Lykke 2022, 20), meaning that in order to stay true to a project's open-ended experimentation, the methods should be articulated after the process, as one looks back at what one has done rather than sticking to something decided beforehand.

Line: I really like that you mention repetition in your take on method. With this project, we are hoping to do something that others might be able to repeat at a later stage, or perhaps more to the point: something they can rethink and reimagine as they see fit, as they might have some completely different takes on it. We are also repeating – to some extent – the work of people we have been inspired by, people have been doing automatic writing before, such as the surrealists.

Katja: Maybe it's worth mentioning in relation to repetition that it implies that something transforms. It's not about doing the same thing twice or many times and expecting it to become the same. To repeat something is to enter new grounds in a way, even transform beyond something that we already know. Conversation is such a method that in the best of worlds is transformative (Ingold 2019).

Line: I think that's a really good point about transformation, and whenever I use the word "repetition", I tend to think of Judith Butler's work on iteration and the performativity of language and the performativity of bodies, and things that we repeat without knowing that we are repeating them, but in that repetition there is also always a difference and a possibility for change (Butler 2011). Nothing can be perfectly copied or repeated. So, yeah, who knows what might happen with the alien toolbox as it is potentially repeated, but with a difference.

Katja: You have already mentioned automatic writing in passing, and we have also covered it in Chapter 1 (this volume). But do you want to add something?

Line: I understand the surrealist's take on automatic writing as a way of trying to get in touch with other, potentially more alien aspects of others and ourselves. That is also what we have been working with, trying to contact the alien, not only as an external figure but as something that's also an inherent part of oneself. There is never this fully developed or understood sense of self, there is always these alien aspects. On a personal note, I'm reminded of Anzaldúa's work, especially the fifth chapter of *Light in the Dark*, where she talks about being blocked and how in order to get out of the block, you need to distract "the editor" (Anzaldúa 2015, 103; see also Chapter 4, this volume). I think conversation is one way to distract it, and automatic writing is another, because you cannot stop editing[a], you have to keep going, and you are not allowed to delete, you are not allowed to stop and think, you just have to keep writing until hopefully, at some point, you reach a subject that you perhaps didn't even know you wanted to write about. That's not necessarily more, like, better, it's not necessarily more profound than something you write from a predefined plan, but it's a space of difference, of the alien, it's trying to find the alien aspects of oneself, those that are a bit of a surprise. It's opening up to the arrival of the alien, that's why we have included the arrival texts that stand before and initiate the chapters where we tell the stories of our encounters with the three figures, slugs (Chapter 2, this volume), diatoms, (Chapter 3 this volume), and familiars (Chapter 4, this volume). We engaged in writing the Arrivals texts, crafted through automatic writing, but also poetically edited, to make space for the alien. We wanted to explore a sense of estrangement and disorientation, that is what drew us to the figure of the alien. So not something in line with the traditional sense of "method" that is about finding a path, going somewhere, so a very goal-oriented process. As it says in the online etymology dictionary, method is "any way of doing anything, orderly regulation of conduct with a view to the attainment of an end". So it's "orderliness", it's "regularity", it's "a system or complete sent [sic] of rules for attaining an end".[1] And I think we are obviously trying to obtain an end, but we are also trying to set ourselves up to be thwarted, to be tripped up a bit, to go astray, to become disoriented and see what emerges in the process.

Katja: Yeah, precisely. We could also say something about why we used automatic writing as method for writing the Alien Arrivals texts (Intertexts I–III). Well, we wanted to explore how we could open up for getting in touch with our respective alien figures. The concrete way that we did this was through diverse poetic, artistic, and multi-sensorial experiments as prompts for the automatic writing. As an example, in one of Nina's prompts, she was reading one of her poems and placing a piece of diatomite on the table ("Alien Arrivals: Diatoms", Intertext II, this volume). This worked as an invitation to pay more close attention in relation to the diatomite, for example, through listening to her poem, and closely looking at, touching, and smelling the diatomite. Our automatic writing was prompted by all this and became the starting point for an imaginative exploration of pathways to get in touch with a piece of diatomite. Another example is one of my prompts, inspired by some of the scientific sensorial aspects of slug biology, namely that slugs do not hear, and they do not see very well, but rather perceive their surroundings through touch, smell, and taste. So I invited us all to sit down outside and take in the moment with earplugs in our ears and closed eyes, and I sprayed small showers of water on the skin of our arms ("Alien Arrivals: Slugs", Intertext I, this volume). This became the starting point for exploring automatic writing as a means of imagining through multi-sensorial dimensions how to become in touch with a slug. I mean, of course, imagined from a human perspective.

Line: Yeah, and I think what is important to me to emphasize is, as you say, that we're doing all this from a human perspective, and we will, therefore, inherently fail figuring out what it means to be a slug. I guess not even a slug would have full access to the experience of being a slug, but as humans, we are even more limited here. To me, the automatic writing methods we used were therefore about trying to open up to alien experiences but also about acknowledging that we will fail – at least if the intention is to know what it's like to be a slug, for example. I kind of like how failure is – again, etymologically – connected to "go[ing] astray".[2] So we were trying to find ways but also knowing that the search was going to fail and, through this failure, open up to the potential of going astray and ending up somewhere completely different. Trying to find that bit of surprise, trying to find that tiny bit of opening up to something we couldn't in any way have predicted in advance, something that would be the alien. This reminds me of Derrida's concept of the "monstrous *arrivant*" (Shildrick 2002, 120), the idea of trying to make space for the other, and especially for the otherness of the other. Though you cannot do that in advance, because you don't know what you are making space for. I don't know how to make space for something that is so other that I cannot imagine it, but I can try to set myself up to fail, and in that failure, perhaps there is a slight disturbance in my perception of the world, a slight bit of "oh, I didn't realize things could be like this", or "this is a surprise". And I think sometimes we managed to surprise ourselves, and sometimes, obviously, the failure doesn't bring anything new with it. Sometimes, it's just frustration, or at least that was my experience. I would just get frustrated, unable to write. So I think with these experiments, you're always taking some risks, and sometimes, you get somewhere, you're getting excited or just somehow *moved*, it's disorienting in interesting ways. But sometimes, you get somewhere, where it's just, like, frustration and annoyance and stuckness, and you need to re-evaluate your methods and tools. Such a re-evaluation is useful and necessary, but also, to me at least, a bit painful at times, because it asks me to change perceptions that I have about myself and my research – perceptions that I do not always want to question. It's an estrangement from the ways I do and have done things, and this is what we've been going for, but, yeah, sometimes just so frustrating. How was your experience?

Katja: Well, I can relate [both laugh].

Line: I still remember the text you wrote for the Mad Meg prompt ("Alien Arrivals: Familiars", Intertext III, this volume), where you wrote this really lovely sentence: "And I have never had so much trouble writing". So I also really want to put it out there, as a part of the alien methodology, that sometimes, the failures and the stuckness weren't generative.

Katja: I think collectivity is an important aspect of this. It helped us to be more courageous in opening up, both to each other and to the aliens and also to the risk of failing. It has often meant that we have supported each other in daring to try things we haven't tried before. We have created a safe space for vulnerability, which, in my opinion, is something that has been crucial to the creative processes and experimentations we did together with our respective alien figures.

Line: Yeah, I think collectivity is definitely such an important part of how we have worked with the alien figures, both through conversation and automatic writing. Ideas don't spring from nothing, knowledge doesn't spring from nothing. You're always in dialogue and conversation with something that has come before, and the collective alien work has made this and not least the more-than-human aspects of collaboration clearer to me. We did not work in the same space all the time – the experimental phase with the prompts and the automatic writing are what we did together, and also the meetings, and the conversations. But we also wrote separately, and in those instances, the collectivity was more spectral, I think, but still present (Prologue, this volume). Like the more spectral aspect of writing, like the ideas of others, internalized voices, the internal editor, and the alien figures, of course. And then there's the wound, this sort of abstract writing companion that has an impact on the process but perhaps in less obvious ways. All three of us have, to some extent, written about and with something that is difficult, maybe even painful.

Katja: Yes, in my case, the wound, in a very concrete sense, was a result of the slug bite, which I write about in Chapter 2 (this volume), which to me became a portal (Akomolafe 2021) to process the idea of becoming in touch with the alien. It became a new realization for me about what it means to really feel the embodied experience of challenging myself as a human, because the slug perceived me as food. The idea of the human as food, it felt like a degradation of the importance of my existence in the world. And it humbled me, and it frightened me, and it challenged my idea of what it means to be human and therefore superior. And that also shifted my romantic idea about more-than-human participatory research (Bastian et al. 2017), about the alien encounter as something that always ends well, something that is always pleasurable, which up to that point was very much my mindset. I had this idea that we all would live in this perfect world where no one was killed and everyone was having a good time.

Line: I think that is part of the alien method and the whole idea about going astray and becoming disoriented and estranged from what you've been taking for granted or not really questioned. Whenever we have been doing this, it is not that we haven't had an idea of what we've wanted to do and some ideas of where we would like things to end up. So we set up these small experiments in the hopes of something happening, of getting some visions of what the world could be without the human at the centre of it. And then something happens which we could not predict, something arrives, we become disoriented, and it's not always great, at least for the human who is removed from the centre of the story.

Katja: Yeah, and Nina recommended me to read the eco-philosopher Val Plumwood's (Plumwood 2012, 9–21) research in relation to her experience of almost being eaten alive by a crocodile, which kind of added another layer to my processing around the slug bite. My whole slug chapter (Chapter 2, this volume) is food oriented – because, you know, the topic of food has been present all the time. But what Plumwood helped me to see was how a human becoming food, me and Plumwood in this case, fundamentally challenges the idea of Western human superiority. To me, this embodied realization of becoming food in relation to the wound as a portal points to something which isn't necessarily meant to be healed but to be stayed with, maybe similar to what Donna Haraway speaks about in her discussion of staying with the trouble (Haraway 2016). This idea of not necessarily seeking closure but actually – in the case of my project with the slugs – to be in this space of accepting that the alien is something other. The slug will always be something completely alien to me, something that I will never understand in the sense that I cannot make sense of it from a human perspective. Instead, I must accept otherness, alienness as a quality to remain unsolved. But what about you and the wound?

Line: Well, I think that, to me, it keeps coming back to etymology. When it comes to the wound, and when it comes to method, I am fascinated by the idea that method, in a 15th-century context, is the "regular, systematic treatment of a disease".[3] Which, if you put that in the context of academic work or anything else then that seems to become the idea that there is some ailment or a wound or an illness or a disease that you have to apply a method to in order to cure it and make it go away – as if the lack of knowledge of something is a disease. Or dis-ease, a lack of ease in the face of not-knowing. In our project, I think we have been going in sort of the opposite direction, not wanting to find ease, not wanting to put something to rest by finally knowing it, but instead trying to make things strange or, as you say, perhaps find ways of living while wounded, living with the wound. Not to romanticize pain, and I think it's important to emphasize that to someone like Anzaldúa (2015), writing is a possible means of healing wounds.

All in all, I find "method" to be a rich word. I also love that it is something that has to do with a pursuit or a following after.[4] We *were* in pursuit, we *were* following after, but we were trying to follow after something we didn't fully know, trying to open up to that pursuit through creative methods such as automatic writing. Instead of curing in the traditional sense of the word, method can be about living with, and instead of going towards an end that you sort of know in advance, it can be about following something strange, and in that following of something strange, becoming estranged one-self, becoming alien through small failures and going astray and becoming disorientated. I think that is what we've been trying to do. Sometimes, it's worked really well, sometimes I've just been sitting there going "nah! I don't know what's happening right now, I cannot write, why am I frustrated?"

Katja: I think you had some good ending sentences there. I think our methods chapter should end on the word "failure".

Joyful Writing

Fur, Denmark
June 2023
Nina, Katja, & Line

Line: For me and Katja, the methods chapter in many ways became a story about our own relationships with writing and some of the struggles that we've had in the writing process. How is *your* relationship with writing, Nina? I know it differs a bit. We had a conversation after you read our draft for the methods chapter, and your initial response was that you have a very different take on writing. Can you perhaps say a few words about that?

Nina: I really like your way of developing the methods chapter through a conversation on vulnerabilities, wounds, and disorientation, and I also really like how you brought writing up in the familiar chapter, Line (Chapter 4, this volume). I definitely think that you are onto something in terms of writing related to vulnerabilities, and to going deeper down into things while exploring vulnerabilities. Especially our automatic writing processes have very much been about going deeper down, because it means skipping the layers of reflection, and just go with the flow, with your thoughts and feelings. So I can follow you in all that, but where I have a different relationship to writing is when it comes to writer's blocks or anxieties about writing.

For me, writing is my way of relaxing. Sometimes, I think it's a bit hard to be with people or doing social things, etc., but when writing, oh, then I can just sculpt my little world. Whether it's a world of feelings and emotions and affects, or if it's a more theoretical version or a mixed-genre text, I find it so relaxing and all absorbing to go there. And the thing is that I found out – especially after writing *Vibrant Death* (Lykke 2022), where I really started to write poetry in a different way than I have been doing earlier, i.e., being more serious about it, so to speak, and also trying to get it published, which represents kind of a threshold – so, after publishing *Vibrant Death*, I found out that I really, really, really love both the poetic and the philosophical writing processes so very much, and I really, really feel totally absorbed and carried away from everything by my writing – apart from Musse [Nina's cat], who would be next to me, while I write, and whose presence gives me much pleasure and catches my attention all the time. But [laugh] beyond Musse. . . . So, yeah, so I really, really feel relaxed about writing. It's the thing I love the most to do, to be with myself and write.

Line: Yeah.

Nina: In a way, I have had it like that always, and I think it goes back to the way I was brought up as a little kid. Because my grandmother, she was a writer and translator. When I met her, she didn't write texts of her own anymore. She had earlier published two novels, but she received some criticism for the last one, which made her stop writing novels. But then she became a translator instead. She translated children's books such as the Swedish author, Astrid Lindgren, but she also translated other kinds of literature and made a living from translating. She took care of me, together with my granddad, until I was seven years old. When I was four years old, my grandmother got a new typewriter, and then she gave me the old one. I think I learned the alphabet when I was, yeah, three/four-ish, and I actually started writing stories when I was four years old. And my grandmother, she was enormously happy and encouraged it, because, I mean, child creativity, that's great! However, another aspect of it was this: "now the child is totally quiet, so I can focus on my work", so my story writing was a win-win situation for both my grandmother and me. So I have always, always, always enjoyed writing very, very, very much.

Katja: Nina, can you say something more about when you use poetry and when you use philosophy or theory? Since our book here is a mixed-genre book, it would be interesting to hear some of your thoughts in relation to why choose one and not the other, so to speak.

Nina: I think these two writing modes – the poetic and the philosophic-theoretic writing modes – are good for different things. I developed my thinking on this when I wrote *Vibrant Death* (Lykke 2022), because, as I said, I had not written poetry or stories in earlier publications. I used to consider myself more of a feminist theorist. But in terms of my reflections in relation to *Vibrant Death*, let me say that, first of all, I did not choose to write *Vibrant Death*, and I did not choose to write it as a mixed-genre book. It just came to me, I had to do it like that because it was part of my mourning. And both sides, both the philosophical and the poetic, were part of my mourning from the start. I think that poetic writing is good for analyzing, capturing, and going deep into the feelings, senses, and corpo-affectivity. Poetry and art can be very good at that, and I do think that it is so important to underline that the artistic-poetic process, dance, or whatever artistic format the process takes is a highly complicated and sophisticated process, as sophisticated and complicated as the philosophical process. So in that sense, in terms of knowledge-making and communicating thoughts, feelings, messages to the world, I consider the two (poetry/art and philosophy/theory) as being on the same level: as equal but good at different things. On the one hand, we have the conceptual work and the conceptual argument, the building that up, and on the other hand, it is about the grasping and the unfolding of corpo-affective aspects – the passions, to tentatively articulate them in emotionally precise words. I see the two writing modes as entangled, but with different kinds of processing and ways of proceeding. I really, really do think that underlining them as equal but different is very important, because there is this hierarchy, at least in the academic world, which I think you react to, Katja, as if theory and philosophy are located "higher" than the other processes. I think that this hierarchizing happens very often when artistic/poetic processes are combined with academic stuff. When the artistic/poetic processes are treated on their own, I think people somehow understand that they are complicated processes. But when they are treated together with the academic side, then they become, "okay, this is just somehow the icing on the cake", or "now you just account for some feelings" or something like that. But when the Danish poet and novelist Naja Marie Aidt, for example, formulated the oxymoron, which I write about (Chapter 5, this volume), it's really a highly, highly, highly philosophical contribution to thinking about life and death. So it's not just a banal statement about "oh, I'm mourning, mourning, mourning", it's instead a highly philosophical-poetic articulation, created by the artistic process, which is so important in terms of creating new knowledge. Like philosophy does it.

Katja: I definitely agree that in a project like our alien encounters project, philosophy, poetry, and art are interlinked. One of the things I think that our book does is to bring in these different genres and show that they are so connected.

Line: I also think that there is a whole history behind it, I mean, creative and academic writing weren't just divided from birth – there has been this whole historical process where poetry was established as more "subjective", and you therefore cannot use it in research, and then scientific language has been established as a specific way of writing that is more "objective", and the two are not meant to mix.

Nina: Yes, I agree very much. The division is a historical construction – a product of Western modernity.

Line: Yeah. So, as part of the alien writing, we have been working with vulnerability as an aspect of the writing process. Is that something you can say a bit more about? Like the role of vulnerability in the writing process and how it's a connecting point between all of our chapters?

Nina: I thought a lot about vulnerability when I wrote the chapter on ethics and aesthetics of this book (Chapter 5, this volume). Like *Vibrant Death* (Lykke 2022) came to me, and the diatoms came to me, and I didn't come to the diatoms (as described in Chapter 3, this volume), it's the same for you two, that the slugs came to you, Katja, you didn't invite them in the first place. Later, you did, but in the first place, you didn't (Chapter 2, this volume). And the same with you and the familiars, Line (Chapter 4, this volume). I also think that it's important that all our three figures came to us in situations where various kinds of vulnerabilities were at stake for us. Because I think that when you are somehow thrown into situations that you really can't control, then you are more open to . . . or perhaps it is more apt to say that in such situations, you can't do things differently because you are not in control. I mean you, Katja, could not have done things differently, when you first encountered the slugs in your garden; I mean, you had to take up this first slug and throw it, and you, Line, somehow had to write with the familiar – or fight or write or whatever you do. There was no controlled choice involved, just spontaneous reaction.

I think that writing in that sense has very much to do with this kind of passionate writing, which somehow throws you into a situation where you cannot do anything but follow the demands of the situation. Though, for me, writing also has very much to do with disidentification: that I feel bothered about something which does not quite fit for me. For example, when we, Katja, had our discussions last year on more-than-human participatory research (Bastian et al. 2017), I said that I felt bothered by or not covered really by the term "research", because what I am doing in relation to the diatoms is not encompassed by the concept of research. So I think writing, for me, is somehow also provoked by this feeling of being bothered; it can be both in f theoretical writing and in more affective writing that I feel bothered, feel prompted to write by something that does not fit. This has also something to do with vulnerability. Because I think when you are bothered, then you're also vulnerable.

Katja: That's interesting, because what you describe now, I realize, is the reason why I came to make the first artwork after the first encounter with the slugs – in my case, it was a video work (Aglert 2007). And then not still feeling totally . . . that there were still some friction, that there were more things triggered from the video that I still had to keep processing, and I continued searching for ways to develop things. Eventually, when I met you, Nina, and you, Line, and Marietta, and we started to engage in this collective writing process of exploring alien encounters together, I felt that writing could actually make me find a new direction, especially automatic writing. It became a way for me to somehow get closer to something I was searching for.

Alien(ated) Writing

Online meeting
June 2023
Katja & Line

Line: When we edited the interview with Nina, it sparked a conversation on how our writing troubles – mine and yours – seem to stem from different things. My own writing anxieties are described in lots of detail in Chapter 4, this volume, but you just now talked a bit about alienation in the context of you as an artist stepping into an academic space, such as this book. I was wondering if you could say a few more words about that, as a way of wrapping up the chapter?

Katja: I think my chain of thought started with how we, in this methods chapter, speak about writing and how we have different positions that we speak from when we speak about writing, as well as different pleasures and anxieties. But I think what is missing for me in the conversation is why you and I came to speak about writing anxiety in the process of the methods chapter from my perspective coming from the arts. It was partly because of the academic writing, which is not necessarily familiar to an artist. I think I expected of myself that I could just do it and took for granted that how to write academically is common knowledge, but it's not.

Line: We had a conversation with Nina, where she talked about dis-identification and being bothered; is that something you can relate to? For her, it was something that propelled her writing, but it also sounds like it can go in the opposite direction and become writing anxiety?

Katja: Yeah, I feel that I was bothered, to use Nina's expression, to the degree where I got some kind of writer's block at first, when we started to write this methods chapter, while still working with the idea to write it in an academic form. But then when you and I got together in my studio and started to play and explore, the block turned into a creative tool, which led to the idea of working in the conversational form. And I have no anxiety about that. That is just fun and creative, and it's a flow. So I think it can go both ways, being bothered can definitely be fuelling, but it can also be a block for creativity, really.

Line: Yeah.

Katja: This process also made me think of something the artist Vito Acconci once said: that spaces inevitably script us and our behav-iour (Acconci 2009). The space of our book is, on the one hand, built from many years of experimentation between artistic, philo-sophical, and poetic practices, and on the other hand, in terms of making our book available to the public, it is adapted into an academic space through the publishing framework of Routledge. Even though we explore the academic publishing space through other forms than academic ones, I think that my writing troubles in relation to the methods chapter is one, for me, telling example of how we can have blind spots in terms of how different spaces script us. In other words, my assumption that I suddenly had to write academically did not come from nowhere but was, in part, a result of the fact that the academic book as a "space" – with its structure of for instance an introductory chapter, a methods chapter, and so on – at first scripted me into thinking that we now had to follow very specific forms of writing. But what is an even more important point to emphasize, I think – especially in a book like ours that engages with vulnerabilities, wounds, and disori-entation through alien encounters and writing practices – is the collective trust we have had throughout the project when it came to open exploration across disciplinary boundaries and making space for the process to guide us. For us, in the work with this methods chapter, that open exploration led us to turning it into a conversation.

Notes

1 Online Etymology Dictionary, s.v. "Method (n.)", accessed July 19, 2023, www.etymonline.com/word/method

2 Online Etymology Dictionary, s.v. "err (v.)", accessed July 19, 2023, www.etymonline.com/search?q=err

3 Online Etymology Dictionary, s.v. "Method (n.)", accessed July 19, 2023, www.etymonline.com/word/method

4 Online Etymology Dictionary, s.v. "Method (n.)", accessed July 19, 2023, www.etymonline.com/word/method

Figure 7.1 Endless End. Collage created for this publication based on photographs by the three authors of this volume.

Source: © Katja Aglert 2023.

Epilogue
Endless End

Nina Lykke, Katja Aglert, and Line Henriksen

This book is the outcome of the actions of two overlapping triquetras. One is composed of three human co-authors, and one is made up of three alien figures whom the humans earlier have encountered in vulnerable situations and whom they have summoned to help them consider how vulnerability can be a portal to alternative sensibilities and worlding practices. Even though both triquetras now, seen in retrospect, look orderly as if pre-planned, we want to underline that the shaping of them has been governed by intuitions rather than specific plans and pre-defined purposes.

The three humans formed a triquetra consciously, insofar as they chose to collaborate. However, from the start, we did not plan to write a book together, and other people than the three humans who appear as co-authors of this volume have been involved along the six-year-long process leading up to it. The book idea emerged spontaneously after the co-authors – in conjunction with different collaborators whom we have thanked in the acknowledgement section – had been doing several workshops on alien encounters. In these workshops, we met different audiences, who received the presentations of our weird companionships with a lot of interest and who also responded enthusiastically to our ways of encouraging them to do automatic writing exercizes and contemplate their own alien encounters. These meetings inspired us and created the intuitive feeling that we could come to even deeper understandings of the implications of a feminist reclaiming of the notion of alien encounters through a shared long-term contemplation that eventually was transformed into this book. For the three alien figures summoned into this book, the process has no doubt been even more intensely governed by spontaneous intuitions, insofar as all the three figures were brought into the triquetra when individually called upon by one of the humans. They did not choose to meet in the book, and as a familiar, summoned in one of our automatic writing exercizes which did not make it into the book, gave us to understand before returning to our shared writing archives: "It is a bit like a blind date to be summoned, you never know what will happen! When you are summoned, you will have to go with the flow of intuitions rather than pre-prepared plans!"

Artistic, poetic, and spiritual intuitions have also been important for the pieces of automatic writing which make up the volume's Alien Arrivals texts (Intertexts I–III) and for the integration of the artworks, including the collages which Katja made specifically for this book. So artistic, poetic, and spiritual intuitions have been important in their own right throughout the book and not as prostheses for its philosophical argument.

However, the book is not only composed through intuitions. It is a mixed-genre book, based on a pursuing of artistic, poetic, and spiritual intuitions but also on philosophical contemplations and articulated purposes. Thus, it has all the way through been a key purpose to make a book that works as an invitation to readers. We offer the book to you who now read this as an invitation and encouragement to start to trace, unfold, or perhaps further develop relationships which you, Reader, already may have with something or someone you experience as alien. We hope that the accounts and reflections on our alien encounters have inspired you to try to envision and summon your own aliens. In case the process of summoning aliens appears exciting and appealing to you, we shall also invite you and your alien/s to consider entering into the alien network, which rhizomatically may unfold beyond our two triquetras if many readers will take up the baton.

We consider our triquetras as a potential start of a network, for which one of our dear collaborators, Chilean curator and artist Camila Marambio, at an extended group meeting some years ago, suggested the term "alie/n/ation". With this notion, Camila wanted us to foreground the collectivity necessary to make estrangement, defamiliarization, and disidentification with human exceptionalism become a global political force that may foster change.

As we have tried to make clear, we think that changes in belief systems and worlding practices are much needed. Modern beliefs in human superiority and exceptionalism, fostered by dualist religions (such as Christianity) and nourished by capitalist technoscientific practices of instrumentalizing bodies (be they human or non-human) as resources for profit extraction, need to be undone, because they put balanced earthly co-habitation and survival in danger. The climate and biodiversity crises and the Anthropocene necropolitics of which they are part testify to the need for change with overwhelming clarity. Human exceptionalist beliefs have created the figure of the alien while alienating the human from the world of which we are part and which we share with so many other critters, human and non-human, dead and alive, organic and inorganic. Alienations made the dichotomous distinctions between us (humans) and not-us (non-humans). As argued (Chapter 5, this volume), the distinctions are products of human thought and should be undone as such.

We consider the alien-work which, in artistic/poetic/philosophical ways, we have argued for and begun with this book as contributions to the critical undoing of the human alienation from the other-than-human world. We have high hopes for a growing alie/n/ation which collectively can accelerate the process of undoing, as well as experiment concretely and affirmatively with altered more-than-human companionships. We think that micropolitical con- creteness is important. To establish an alternative relation to an alien figure and contemplate the undoing of exceptionalism and human alienation through such a more-than-human companionship may seem to be a very small thing compared to the enormous task of un- and redoing human relationships with the more-than-human world at large. However, the process of alie/n/ation- building needs to grow from below, following the letting-thousand-flowers- flower principle. It cannot be ordered from above.

But let us also underline that claiming the importance of action from below does not in any way free governments and international organizations from their obligation to take macropolitical responsibility for necessary changes from above. We believe that the process of undoing human exceptionalism can only happen as a result of millions and millions of micro-political acts such as the ones we have discussed in this book. But it is important for the rhizomatic spread of the work of un- and redoing from below that overall, macropolitically shaped infrastructures support rather than impede such a spread.

While sitting surrounded by Nina's beloved diatomaceous Fur cliffs towards the end of our work on the book, we took a round on what we have learnt from the process. The most important themes were creative intuition, mixed- genre writing, collectivity, and an ethico-political invitation to the reader to engage in alien work and embrace the affirmative alie/n/ation-building from their own perspectives. To make ourselves accountable for what we – the three co-authors – learnt from the writing process, we also concluded that it was important to be aware of the ways in which alien work requires new sensibilities and a willingness to enter into chaos, to investigate rather than shy away from feelings of vulnerability, and to be open to adventure and the unexpected. We agreed that Donna Haraway's formula that it is important to "stay with the trouble" (2016) summarizes well the approach to alien work, which we had come to consider as important through our collective reflections on our processes of alien encounters.

However, while contemplating what we learnt from the encounters with the alien figures and from our shared reflections on them, we kept returning to the power of intuitions, that is: the ways in which artistic, poetic, and spiritual intuitions had guided us, both individually and collectively. To keep believing in one's intuitions and to follow them through in an artistic, poetic, and/or spiritual process and to support each other in not giving up but to pursue further and further the stories of the weird companionships on which the book is based were strongly foregrounded by all of us.

Therefore, to pay respect to the power of intuitive, artistic, and do-it-yourself-spiritual processes, which guided us, we will create an endless end – an end which can be endlessly continued by readers who want to engage in alien conversations. The following text is made of snippets from an Alien Q&A into which we (the humans) tried to summon the three aliens to help us articulate an endless end that can work as a new beginning for readers interested in alien work.

Alien Q&A

Dear S.

Forgive me for asking a question which to you, S., may seem banal, trivial, or too personal, only for non-humans to discuss. But I so much would like to know if you enjoy the companionship of other slugs, and if yes, when is the pleasure to be with another slug most intense? I ask because, for years, I have been so enchanted by the intensity of the passionate fleshy encounter of your snail cousins in the documentary film *Microcosmos. Le Peuple de l'Herbe* by French biologists Nuridsany and Pérennou (1996).
Love/N.

Dear N.

Hhhhhhhhhhhrrrrrrrrrrrmmmmpppppppppppffffffffffffffff, oooooooooohhhhhhhhhh well, since you're asking so humidly – sorry, humbly. Though, I have to admit I am quite busy these days finding a safe place when the season turn hostile for a slug like myself. I'm sure you've heard of the expression "lone wolf". Well, "lone slug" would be more appropriate, as wolves, according to my knowledge, enjoy being in company of others. I do not enjoy the companionship of other slugs. Like yourself, I have been delighted to watch snails (live from hidden sight) many times when they dance in intense moist, passionate encounters. However, I do what I can to avoid slimy encounters. There are several reasons for this, and I will share with you one of them: the risk of being robbed of my slime. Our kin the snails can afford the pleasures of companionships in life because they can store slime in their shells. A slug, as you might know, stores a slime nugget on the back in the open. Never safe. So far, bound to solitude. However, I will tell you a secret. In late nights, I have glided into homes of human beings and slid onto their touchscreens and watched You-Tube clips from BBC. Oh, Hermit Crabs! Have you seen how they naked climb out of and into empty shells and cans that they encounter, wearing them as both protection, home, and dress? What an inspiration!
With a lot of hungry love-bites/S.

Dear D.

My question is short, although not simple: How is it to be a free-floating creature that later becomes "stuck" in the cliffs of the Fur Formation? What ghost stories can be told about cliffs?

Hugs/L.

Dear L.

Oh, you know, being both free-floating and stationary is a great way to try out different modes and moods of being. Oysters and mussels do almost the same thing, but within one lifetime. Their larvae float, and later, they find a place to be stationary and grow big. It is also somehow like trying out what two other branches of my kin do – animals move around, while terrestrial plants root, even the ones that have the capability to spread rhizomatically need to root. As we – diatoms – are in-between these two kinds of planetary kin – being both animal-like with an urea cycle and plant-like, doing photosynthesis, this may also have contributed to our desires to try out both these modes and moods of being. That we do it so that we are free-floating in life while sedimenting and becoming stationary in death does not matter so much as these other reasons. I mean: Who cares about the difference between life and death anyway? We are vibrant no matter what – in life, in death, as spectres! If you visit me again, I'll tell you a story about my ancestors who wanted to appear as the ghost of a giant and who succeeded. Because even though they were all microscopic, they were also enormously patient and visionary, so having pulled their microscopic corpses together through millions of years, in the end, they came to jointly appear as the tooth of a giant, and what a feast they had when it happened.

Don't hesitate to contact me again if you have more questions/D

Dear F.

With your advanced experience of night life and knowledge about food, I cannot think of anyone better to ask. I hope you don't mind me reaching out to you. I am planning to throw a soirée and would like to offer my guests a selection of snacks that can take the heat. Do you have any tips? Thank you for your consideration.

Warmly, K.

Dear K.

Souls. With melted cheese. Personally, I'd go for a light to medium sin-bouquet so as not to overwhelm the guests with too rich a taste early on. Maybe the souls of people who don't cover their mouths when they sneeze or who eat crackers in library reading halls. The cheese should be donated by a cow with a dark secret or who has at the very least stood on someone's foot for 12 minutes or more, deliberately and without moving. As the night progresses, I suggest more seasoned souls, such as those of directors of banks or the person living in the flat next to me, who plays the same song day and night, loud and on repeat (it's "Hello" by Adele). Anyway. At this point, the cheese should be donated by a cow skilled in the Dark Arts. You can find a register of practicing Satanic Cows in your local area in my cookbook "Cook Your Neighbour. You'll Like It".

I wish you a wonderful evening/F

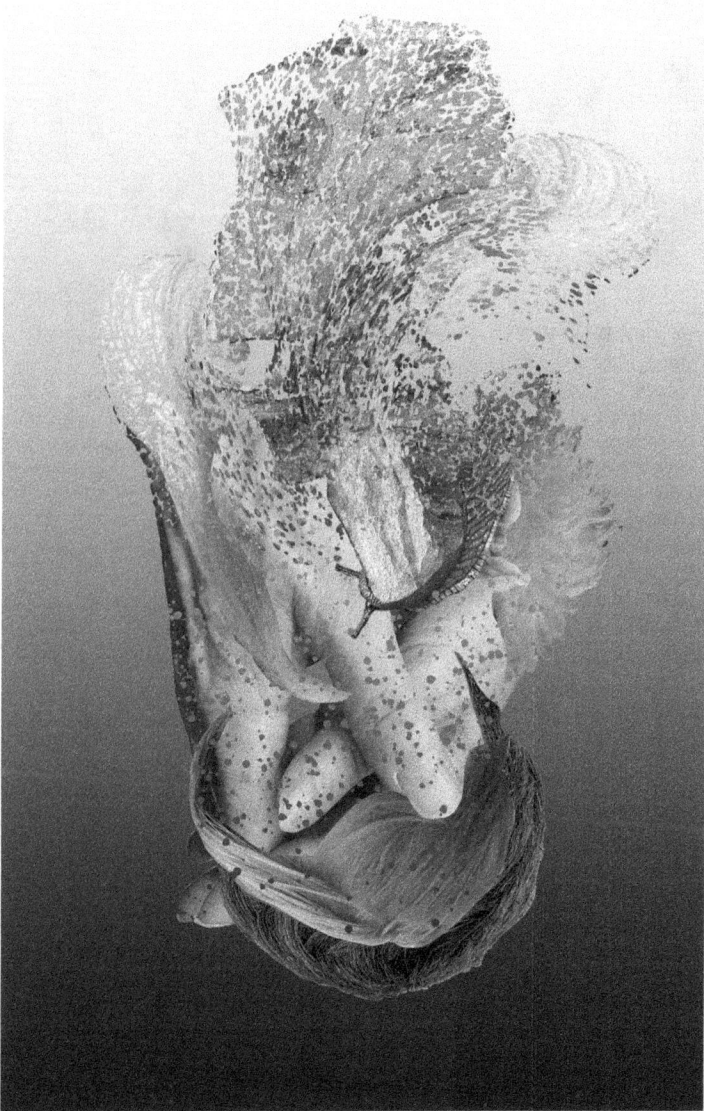

Figure 7.2 Endless End – Invitation. Collage created for this publication based on photographs by the three authors of this volume.

Source: © Katja Aglert and Oskar Aglert 2023.

References

Acampora, Ralph R. 2006. *Corporal Compassion: Animal Ethics and Philosophy of Body*. Pittsburgh, PA: Pittsburgh University Press.

Acconci, Vito, and Hans Ulrich Obrist. "Vito Acconci & Hans Ulrich Obrist in conversation". *Public conversation organized in the context of Unbuilt Roads, e-flux, New York*, May 12, 2009. Accessed June 29, 2023. www.e-flux.com/live/65422/vito-acconci-amp-hans-ulrich-obrist-in-conversation/.

Aglert, Katja, dir. 2007. *Momentary Seizures*. Filmform.

Aidt, Naja Marie. 2019. *When Death Takes Something from You, Give It Back – Carl's Book*. Translated by Denise Newman. Minneapolis, MN: Coffee House Press.

Akomolafe, Bayo, guest. 2021. "Slowing Down and Surrendering Human Centrality." *Green Dreamer* (podcast), July 20, 2021. Accessed July 20, 2023. https://greendreamer.com/podcast/dr-bayo-akomolafe-the-emergence-network

Allen, Andrew E., Christopher L. Dupont, Miroslav Oborník, Aleš Horák, Adriano Nunes-Nesi, John P. McCrow, Hong Zheng, Daniel A. Johnson, Hanhua Hu, Alisdair R. Fernie, and Chris Bowler. 2011. "Evolution and Metabolic Significance of the Urea Cycle in Photosynthetic Diatoms." *Nature* 473 (7346): 203–207. https://doi.org/10.1038/nature10074.

Anzaldúa, Gloria E. 2015. *Light in the Dark/Luz en Lo Oscuro: Rewriting Identity, Reality, Spirituality*. Durham, NC: Duke University Press.

Bachofen, Johann Jakob. [1861] 1967. *Myth, Religion and Mother Right*. Translated by Ralph Manheim. Princeton, NJ: Princeton University Press.

Bailey, Elisabeth Tova. 2010. *The Sound of a Wild Snail Eating*. Chapel Hill, NC: Algonquin Books.

Barr, Marlene S. 1993. *Lost in Space: Probing Feminist Science Fiction and Beyond*. London and Chapel Hill, NC: University of North Carolina Press.

Bastian, Michelle. 2017. "Towards a More-than-Human Participatory Research." In *Participatory Research in More-than-Human Worlds*, edited by Michelle Bastian, Owain Jones, Niamh Moore and Emma Roe, 19–37. London: Routledge.

Bastian, Michelle, Owain Jones, Niamh Moore, and Emma Roe, ed. 2017. *Participatory Research in More-than-Human Worlds*. London: Routledge.

Bennett, Jane. 2010. *Vibrant Matter: A Political Ecology of Things*. Durham, NC and London: Duke University Press.

Bergold, Jarg, and Stefan Thomas. 2012. "Participatory Research Methods: A Methodological Approach in Motion." *FQS Forum: Qualitative Social Research* 13 (1). https://doi.org/10.17169/fqs-13.1.1801.

Black, Christine F. 2018. *A Mosaic of Indigenous Legal Thought: Legendary Tales and Other Writings*. New York: Routledge.

Boland, Yasmin. 2018. *Moonology Oracle Cards*. London: Hay House.

Bonde, Niels. 2008. "Osteoglossomorphs of the Marine Lower Eocene of Denmark – With Remarks on Other Eocene Taxa and their Importance for Palebiogeography." In *Fishes and the Break-Up of Pangaea*, vol. 295, edited by Lionel Cavin, Alison Longbottom and Martha Richter, 253–310. Geological Society, London: Special Publications. https://doi.org/10.1144/SP295.

Braidotti, Rosi. 2006. *Transpositions: On Nomadic Ethics*. Cambridge: Polity Press.

Brecht, Bertolt. 1964. *Brecht on Theatre. The Development of an Aesthetic*. Edited and Translated by J. Willett. London: Eyre Methuen.

Breton, André. 1971. *Manifestos of Surrealism*. Ann Arbor: University of Michigan Press.

Bryld, Mette, and Nina Lykke. 2000. *Cosmodolphins. Feminist Cultural Studies of Technology, Animals and the Sacred*. London: ZED Books.

Burroway, Janet. 2014. *Imaginative Writing*. Boston: Pearson.

Butler, Judith. 2011. *Bodies that Matter: On the Discursive Limits of "Sex"*. New York: Routledge.

Butler, Octavia E. 1987. *Dawn*. New York, NY: Warner.

Castro-Gómez, Santiago. 2021. *Zero-Point Hubris. Science, Race and Enlightenment in Eighteenth Century Latin America*. Translated by George Ciccariello-Maher and Don T. Deere. Lanham, MD: Rowman & Littlefield.

Cixous, Hélène. 1991. "Coming to Writing." In *Hélène Cixous: Coming to Writing and Other Essays*, edited and translated by Deborah Jenson, 1–59. Cambridge, MA: Harvard University Press.

Conley, Katherine. 2016. "The Surrealist Collection: Ghosts in the Laboratory." In *A Companion to Dada and Surrealism*, edited by David Hopkins, 304–318. Chichester, Malden and Oxford: Wiley-Blackwell.

Crist, Eileen. 2013. "On the Poverty of Our Nomenclature." *Environmental Humanities* 3 (1): 129–147. https://doi.org/10.1215/22011919-3611266.

Curman, Sofia, and Zamora, Paola. 2007. "Introduction to the video Momentary Seizures by Katja Aglert.". Stockholm: "konstbio". Pamphlet for the screening program *Provocateurs?*

de la Cadena, Marisol. 2015. "Uncommoning Nature." In *e-flux*. Venice: 56th Venice Biennale.

de la Cadena, Marisol, and Mario Blaser. 2018. *A World of Many Worlds*. Durham: Duke University Press.

Deleuze, Gilles. 2020. *Logic of Sense*. Translated by Constantin V. Boundas, Mark Lester and Charles J. Stivale. London: Bloomsbury.

Deleuze, Gilles, and Felix Guattari. 1988. *A Thousand Plateaus: Capitalism and Schizophrenia*. Translated by Brian Massumi. New York, NY and London: Continuum.

———. 1994. *What is Philosophy?* Translated by Graham Burchell and Hugh Tomlinson. New York: Columbia University Press.

Derrida, Jacques. 1994. *Specters of Marx: The State of the Debt, the Work of Mourning and the New International*. Translated by Peggy Kamuf. New York, NY and London: Routledge.

———. 2002. "The Animal That Therefore I Am (More to follow) (Translated by David Wills)." *Critical Inquiry* 28 (2): 369–418.

———. 2008. *The Animal that Therefore I am (More to follow).* Translated by David Wills. New York, NY: Fordham University Press.

Ejstrud, Jannie Uhre, and Birgit Christensen. 2018. "Vitterlige troldfolk: – trolddom og trolddomsangst i to hekseprocesser fra Sydøstjylland i 1620." *By, marsk og geest – Kulturhistorisk tidsskrift for Sydvestjylland* 30 (1): 31–59.

European Environment Agency. 2009. "Killer Slugs and Other Aliens – Europe's Biodiversity is Disappearing at an Alarming Rate." May 11, 2021. Accessed June 2, 2023. www.eea.europa.eu/articles/killer-slugs-and-other-aliens

Falconer, Rachel. 2010. "Hell in Our Time: Dantean Descent and the Twenty-First Century 'War on Terror.'" In *Hell and Its Afterlife: Historical and Contemporary Perspectives,* edited by Isabel Moreira and Margaret Toscano, 217–236. Surrey and Burlington: Ashgate.

Federici, Silvia. 2004. *Caliban and the Witch. Women, the Body and Primitive Accumulation.* Brooklyn, NY: Autonomedia.

Ferrando, Francesca. 2016. "A Feminist Genealogy of Posthuman Aesthetics in the Visual Arts." *Palgrave Communications.* https://doi.org/10.1057/palcomms.2016.11.

France, Kim, and Jennifer Romolini, hosts. 2023. "Living 'The Artist's Way' – With Julia Cameron!" *Everything is Fine* (podcast), January 30, 2023. Accessed 30 May, 2023. https://shows.acast.com/everythingisfine/episodes/living-the-artists-way-with-julia-cameron.

Glissant, Édouard. 2012. *Relationens filosofi: omfångets poesi.* Translated by Christina Kullberg and Johan Sehlberg. Göteborg: Glänta produktion.

Goettner-Abendroth, Heide. 2012. *Matriarchal Societies. Studies on Indigenous Cultures Across the Globe.* Translated by Karen Smith. New York, NY: Peter Lang.

Gorey, Edward. 1980. "The Disrespectful Summons." In *Amphigorey Too.* New York, NY: Penguin.

Göttner-Abendroth, Heide. (1980). *Die Göttin und ihr Heros: Die matriarchalen Religionen in Mythos, Märchen und Dichting.* München: Frauenoffensive.

Graves, Robert. 1961. *The White Goddess. A Historical Grammar of Poetic Myth.* London: Faber and Faber.

Haeckel, Ernst. [1904] 2000. *Kunstformen der Natur/Artforms in Nature* (Dover Pictorial Archive). Mineola, NY: Dover Publications.

Hagen, Sofie, dir. 2023. "Sofie Hagen & French Brutus | Body Confidence." *YouTube,* 2023. www.youtube.com/watch?v=6R8KAjlShNw.

Hallegraeff, Gustaaf, Henrik Enevoldsen, and Adriana Zingone. 2021. "Global Harmful Algal Bloom Status Reporting." *Harmful Algae* 102. https://doi.org/10.1016/j.hal.2021.101992.

Haraway, Donna. 2008. *When Species Meet.* Minneapolis, MN: University of Minnesota Press.

———. 2016. *Staying with the Trouble, Making Kin in the Chthulucene.* Durham: Duke University Press.

Hazekamp, Risk, and Nina Lykke. 2022. "Ancestral Conviviality. How I Fell in Love with Queer Critters". *Forum+* 29 (3): 30–36. https://doi.org/10.5117/FORUM2022.3.008.HAZE.

Henriksen, Line, Katrine Meldgaard Kjær, Marie Blønd, Marisa Cohn, Baki Cakici, Rachel Douglas-Jones, Pedro Ferreira, Viktoriya Feshak, Simy Kaur Gahoonia, and Sunniva Sandbukt. 2021. "Writing Bodies and Bodies of Text: Thinking Vulnerability through Monsters." *Gender, Work & Organization* 29 (2): 561–74. https://doi.org/10.1111/gwao.12782.

Holmberg, Tora. 2013. "Trans-Species Urban Politics: Stories From a Beach." *Space and Culture* 16 (1): 28–42. https://doi.org/10.1177/1206331212452365.

Holmberg, Tora, and Katja Aglert. 2017. "Open Endings." In *Urban Animals, Crowding in Zoocities*, edited by Tora Holmberg, 128–145. London and New York: Routledge.

Ingold, Timothy. "Sustainability of Everything." Lecture at *The Transformative Imagination, Moderna Museet, Stockholm*, September 17, 2019. Accessed October 30, 2023. https://www.modernamuseet.se/stockholm/en/event/the-transformative-imagination/.

Irish Around the World. 2023. *Triquetra & Trinity Knot Symbol: Meanings and History*. Accessed July 31, 2023. https://irisharoundtheworld.com/triquetra-trinity-knot/.

Jackson, Zakiyyah Iman. 2020. *Becoming Human. Matter and Meaning in an Antiblack World*. New York, NY: New York University Press.

Johansen, Jens Christian V. 1991. *Da Djævelen Var Ude . . . – Trolddom i Det 17. Århundredes Danmark*. Odense: Odense Universitetsforlag.

Jakobson, Roman. 1987. *Language in Literature*. Edited by Krystyna Pomorska and Stephen Rudy. Cambridge, MA: Harvard University Press.

Kallestrup, Louise Nyholm. 2009. *I Pagt Med Djævelen. Trolddomsforfølgelser og Trolddomsforestillinger i Danmark Og Italien i Den Post-Reformatoriske Periode*. København: Forlaget Anis.

Koobak, Redi. 2014. "Six Impossible Things Before Breakfast: How I Came Across My Research Topic and What Happened Next." In *Writing Academic Texts Differently Intersectional Feminist Methodologies and the Playful Art of Writing*, edited by Nina Lykke, 95–110. London and New York: Routledge.

Kristeva, Julia. 1982. *Powers of Horror: An Essay on Abjection*. Translated by Leon S. Roudiez. New York, NY: Columbia University Press.

Leavy, Patricia. 2016. *Fiction as Research Practice: Short Stories, Novellas, and Novels*. New York: Routledge.

Lie, Sissel. 2014. "From an Empty Head to a Finished Text. The Writing Process." In *Writing Academic Texts Differently Intersectional Feminist Methodologies and the Playful Art of Writing*, edited by Nina Lykke, 126–141. London and New York: Routledge.

Lykke, Nina. 2010. *Feminist Studies: A Guide to Intersectional Theory, Methodology and Writing*. New York and London: Routledge.

———, ed. 2014. *Writing Academic Texts Differently. Intersectional Feminist Methodologies and the Playful Art of Writing*. London and New York: Routledge.

———. 2018. "Passionately Posthuman. From Feminist Disidentifications to Postdisciplinary Posthumanities." In *Feminist Companion to the Posthumanities*, edited by Cecilia Åsberg and Rosi Braidotti, 23–35. Berlin and New York: Springer International Publishing.

———. 2019a. "Co-Becoming with Algae: Between Posthuman Mourning and Wonder in Algae Research." *Catalyst: Feminism, Theory, Technoscience* 5 (2). https://doi.org/10.28968/cftt.v5i2.31922.

———. 2019b. "Making Live and Letting Die: Cancerous Bodies between Anthropocene Necropolitics and Chthulucene Kinship." *Environmental Humanities* 11 (1): 108–36. https://doi.org/10.1215/22011919-7349444.

———. 2022. *Vibrant Death. A Posthuman Phenomenology of Mourning*. London: Bloomsbury.

———. Forthcoming a. "Contemplating Suffocation through the Lens of Shared Cross-species Vulnerabilities." In *Social and Political Suffocations*, edited by Magda Górska and Milica Trakilovic. London and New York: Routledge.

———. Forthcoming b. "Poetic Posthumanities: Art/Poetry/Research." In *Posthuman Convergences: Reflections on Methods and Practices*, edited by Goda Klumbytė, Emily Jones and Rosi Braidotti. Edinburgh: Edinburgh University Press.

———. Forthcoming c. "Between Molar, Molecular and Spectral Mourning. Contemplating Death and Mourning. Differently." In *Subjectivity, Embodiment, Agency. At the Intersection of Phenomenology and Feminist Technoscience*, edited by Lisa Käll and Kristin Zeiler. Durham, NC: Duke University Press.

———. Forthcoming d. "Contemplating Life, Death and Time Together with Diatoms." In *Being Algae. Critical Plant Studies Series*, edited by Johanna Weggelaar, Sergio Mugnai, Natalia de Rossi and Yogi Hendlin. Leiden: Brill Publishers.

MacCormack, Patricia. 2020. *The Ahuman Manifesto. Activism for the End of the Anthropocene*. London: Bloomsbury Academic.

MacLure, Maggie. 2021. "Inquiry as Divination." *Qualitative Inquiry* 27 (5): 502–511. https://doi.org/10.1177/1077800420939124.

Mbembe, Achille. 2003. "Necropolitics." *Public Culture* 15 (1): 11–40.

National Oceanic and Atmospheric Administration. 2022. "What is Harmful Algal Bloom?" *NOOAS, US Department of Commerce*. Accessed June 5, 2022. www.noaa. gov/what-is-harmful-algal-bloom.

Neimanis, Astrida. 2017. *Bodies of Water: Posthuman Feminist Phenomenology*. London and New York, NY: Bloomsbury Academic.

Nielsen, Michael Lerche. 2018. "Gelster, Register og andre djævlenavne." *Københavns Universitet*, June 1, 2018. Accessed 20 July, 2021. https://navn.ku.dk/maanedens_navn/gelster-register-og-andre-djaevlenavne/.

Nuridsany, Claude, and Marie Pérennou. 1996. *Microcosmos. Le Peuple de l'Herbe*. Levallois-Perret: Galatée Films.

Pedersen, Gunvor Krarup. 1981. "Anoxic Events During Sedimentation of a Palaeogene Diatomite in Denmark." *Sedimentology* 28: 487–504.

Pitt, Hannah. 2017. "An Apprenticeship in Plant Thinking." In *Participatory Research in More-than-Human Worlds*, edited by Michelle Bastian, Owain Jones, Niamh Moore and Emma Roe, 92–106. London: Routledge.

Plumwood, Val. 1993. *Feminism and the Mastery of Nature*. London and New York: Routledge.

Plumwood, Val. 2012. "Meeting the Predator." In *The Eye of the Crocodile*, edited by Lorraine Shannon, 9–22. Canberra: Australian National University E-Press.

Plumwood, Val, and Shannon, Lorraine. 2012. *The Eye of the Crocodile*. Canberra: Australian National University E-Press.

Povinelli, Elizabeth A. 2016. *Geontologies. A Requien to Late Liberalism*. Durham, NC: Duke University Press.

Radomska, Marietta. 2020. "Deterritorialising Death: Queerfeminist Biophilosophy and Ecologies of the Non/Living." *Australian Feminist Studies* 35 (104): 116–137. https://doi.org/10.1080/08164649.2020.1802697.

Radomska, Marietta, Tara Mehrabi, and Nina Lykke. 2020. "Queer Death Studies. Death, Dying and Mourning from a Queerfeminist Perspective." *Australian Feminist Studies* 35 (104): 81–100. https://doi.org/10.1080/08164649.2020.1811952.

Rieder, John. 2008. *Colonialism and the Emergence of Science Fiction*. Middleton, CT: Wesleyan University Press.

Rose, Deborah Bird. 2012. "Multispecies Knots of Ethical Time." *Environmental Philosophy* 9(1): 127–140.

———. 2017. "Monk Seals at the Edge. Blessings in a Time of Peril." In *Extinction Studies. Stories of Times, Death and Generations*, edited by Deborah Bird Rose, Thom van Dooren and Matthew Chrulew, 116–146. New York: Colombia University Press.

Rosemont, Penelope, ed. 1998. *Surrealist Women: An International Anthology*. Austin, TX: University of Texas Press.

Rowson, Ben, James Turner, Roy Anderson, and Bill Symondson. 2014. *Slugs of Britain and Ireland. Identification, Understanding and Control*. Totnes: Field Studies Council.

Schaeffer, Felicity Amaya. 2018. "Spirit Matters: Gloria Anzaldúa's Cosmic Becoming across Human/Nonhuman Borderlands." *Signs: Journal of Women in Culture and Society* 43(4): 1005–1029. https://doi.org/10.1086/696630.

Schrader, Astrid. 2012. "The Time of Slime: Anthropocentrism in Harmful Algal Research." *Environmental Philosophy* 9 (1): 71–94.

Sharma, Vallabh P. 1969. "Early Tertiary Field Reversals Recorded in Volcanic Ash Layers of Northern Denmark." *Bulletin of the Geological Society of Denmark* 19: 218–223.

Shildrick, Margrit. 2002. *Embodying the Monster: Encounters with the Vulnerable Self*. London: Sage.

Shklovsky, Viktor. 1990. *Theory of Prose*. Translated by Benjamin Sher. Elmwood Park, IL: Dalkey Archive Press.

St. Pierre, Elizabeth Adams. 2018. "Writing Post Qualitative Inquiry." *Qualitative Inquiry* 24 (9): 603–608. https://doi.org/10.1177/1077800417734567.

Sullivan, Margaret A. 2010. *Bruegel and the Creative Process, 1559–1563*. Surrey: Ashgate.

Suvin, Darko. 1979. *Metamorphoses of Science Fiction: On the Poetics and History of a Literary Genre*. New Haven, CT: Yale University Press.

The Monster Network. 2021. "Collective Voices and the Materialisation of Ideas: The Monster as Methods." In *Monstrous Ontologies: Politics, Ethics, Materiality*, edited by Caterina Nirta and Andrea Pavoni, 143–167. Malaga: Vernon Press.

Tiffany, Mary Ann, and Nagy Stephen S. 2019. "The Beauty of Diatoms." In *Diatoms: Fundamentals and Applications*, edited by Joseph Seckbach and Richard Gordon, 33–43. Hoboken, NJ: Wiley, and Beverly: Scrivener.

Tlostanova, Madina. 2023. "Can Methodologies be Decolonial? Towards a Relational Experiential Epistemic Togetherness." In *Pluriversal Conversations on Transnational Feminisms: And Words Collide from a Place*, edited by Nina Lykke, Redi Koobak, Petra Bakos, Swati Arora and Kharnita Mohamed. London: Routledge.

Tlostanova, Madina, and Walter Mignolo. 2009. "On Pluritopic Hermeneutics, Trans-Modern Thinking, and Decolonial Philosophy." *Encounters* 1 (1): 11–27.

———. 2012. *Learning to Unlearn: Decolonial Reflections from Eurasia and the Americas*. Columbus, OH: Ohio State University Press.

Todd, Zoe. 2016. "An Indigenous Feminist's Take on the Ontological Turn: 'Ontology' Is Just Another Word for Colonialism." *Journal of Historical Sociology* 29 (1): 4–22.

Treusch, Pat. 2017. "Re-reading ELIZA: Human-machine Interaction as Cognitive Sense-ability." *Australian Feminist Studies* 32 (94): 411–426.

Tsing, Anna Lowenhaupt, Bubandt, Nils, Gan, Elaine, and Swanson, Anne Heather, eds. 2017. *Arts of Living on a Damaged Planet. Ghosts and Monsters of the Anthropocene*. Minneapolis, MN: University of Minnesota Press.

Vendetti, Jann. n.d. "A Microscopic Look at Snail Jaws." Natural History Museum, Los Angeles County website. Accessed June 29, 2023. https://nhm.org/stories/microscopic-look-snail-jaws.

von Proschwitz, Ted, Kennet Lundin, Jonas Roth, and Robert Back. 2023. *Blötdjur: Snyltsnäckor-skivsnäckor. Mollusca Pyramidellidae-Planorbidae.* Uppsala: Nationalnyckeln till Sveriges flora och fauna/SLU Artdatabanken.

Walker, Barbara G. 1988. *The Women's Dictionary of Symbols & Sacred Objects.* San Francisco: Harper & Row Publishers.

Walter, Beth A. 2014. "Communication and Response-ability: Levinas and Kierkegaard in Conversation." Doctoral diss., Duquesne University. https://dsc.duq.edu/etd/1330.

Wikipedia. 2023a. *Diatoms.* Accessed February 1, 2023. https://en.wikipedia.org/wiki/Diatom.

Wikipedia. 2023b. *Triquetra.* Accessed July 31, 2023. https://en.wikipedia.org/wiki/Triquetra.

Williams, Peter. 2009. *Snail.* London: Reaktion Books.

Yusoff, Kathryn. 2018. *A Billion Black Anthropocenes or None.* Minneapolis, MN: University of Minnesota Press.

Index

126 *Index*

For Product Safety Concerns and Information please contact our EU
representative GPSR@taylorandfrancis.com
Taylor & Francis Verlag GmbH, Kaufingerstraße 24, 80331 München, Germany